SELECT COMMITTEE TO INVESTIGATE THE
JANUARY 6TH
ATTACK ON THE UNITED STATES CAPITOL

Seventh Select Committee Hearing
July 12, 2022

COMPLETE TRANSCRIPT

THE JANUARY 6TH REPORT

# # #

<u>Bennie Thompson</u>: "The Select Committee to investigate the January 6th attack on the United States Capitol will be in order. Without objection, the chair is authorized to declare the committee in recess at any point. Pursuant to House Deposition Authority Regulation 10, the chair announces the committee's approval to release the deposition material presented during today's hearing.

"Good afternoon. When I think about the most basic way to explain the importance of elections in the United States, there's a phrase that always comes to mind. It may sound straightforward, but it's meaningful. We settle our differences at the ballot box. Sometimes my choice prevails, sometimes yours does, but it's that simple.

"We cast our votes. We count the votes. If something seems off with the results, we can challenge them in court, and then we accept the results. When you're on the losing side, that doesn't mean you have to be happy about it. And in the United States, there's plenty you can do and say so. You can protest.

"You can organize. You can get ready for the next election to try to make sure your side has a better chance the next time the people settle their differences at the ballot box. But you can't turn violent. You can't try to achieve your desired outcome through force or harassment or intimidation. Any real leader who sees their supporters going down that path, approaching that line has a responsibility to say stop, we gave it our best, we came up short, we try again next time, because we settle our differences at the ballot box.

"On December 14th, 2020, the presidential election was officially over. The Electoral College had cast its vote. Joe

Biden was the president elect of the United States. By that point, many of Donald Trump's supporters were already convinced that the election had been stolen because that's what Donald Trump had been telling them.

"So, what Donald Trump was required to do in that moment, what would have been required of any American leader, was to say we did our best and we came up short. He went the opposite way. He seized on the anger he had already stoked among his most loyal supporters. And as they approached the line, he didn't wave them off.

"He urged them on. Today the committee will explain how, as a part of his last ditch effort to overturn the election and block the transfer of power, Donald Trump summoned a mob to Washington DC and ultimately spurred that mob to wage a violent attack on our democracy. Our colleagues, Ms. Murphy of Florida and Mr. Raskin of Maryland, will lay out this story.

"First, I'm pleased to recognize our distinguished vice chair, Ms. Cheney of Wyoming, for any opening comments she'd care to offer."

Liz Cheney: "Thank you very much, Mr. Chairman. Our committee did not conduct a hearing last week, but we did conduct an on the record interview of President Trump's former White House counsel, Pat Cipollone. If you've watched these hearings, you've heard us call for Mr. Cipollone to come forward to testify. He did, and Mr. Cipollone's testimony met our expectations.

"We will save for our next hearing President Trump's behavior during the violence of January 6th. Today's hearing will take us from December 14th, 2020, when the Electoral College met and certified the results of the 2020 presidential election, up through the morning of January 6th. You will see certain segments of Pat Cipollone's testimony today. We will also see today how President

Trump summoned a mob to Washington and how the president's stolen election lies provoked that mob to attack the Capitol. And we will hear from a man who was induced by President Trump's lies to come to Washington and join the mob and how that decision has changed his life.

"Today's hearing is our seventh. We have covered significant ground over the past several weeks, and we have also seen a change in how witnesses and lawyers in the Trump orbit approach this committee. Initially, their strategy in some cases appeared to be to deny and delay. Today there appears to be a general recognition that the committee has established key facts, including that virtually everyone close to President Trump, his Justice Department officials, his White House advisers, his White House counsel, his campaign, all told him the 2020 election was not stolen.

"This appears to have changed the strategy for defending Donald Trump. Now the argument seems to be that President Trump was manipulated by others outside the administration, that he was persuaded to ignore his closest advisers, and that he was incapable of telling right from wrong. This new strategy is to try to blame only John Eastman or Sidney Powell or Congressman Scott Perry or others and not President Trump.

"In this version, the president was 'poorly served' by these outside advisers. The strategy is to blame people his advisers called 'the crazies' for what Donald Trump did. This, of course, is nonsense. President Trump is a 76 year old man. He is not an impressionable child. Just like everyone else in our country, he is responsible for his own actions and his own choices.

"As our investigation has shown, Donald Trump had access to more detailed and specific information showing that the election was not actually stolen than almost any other American, and he was told this over and over again. No rational or sane man in his position could disregard that information and reach the opposite conclusion.

"And Donald Trump cannot escape responsibility by being willfully blind, nor can any argument of any kind excuse President Trump's behavior during the violent attack on January 6th. As you watch our hearing today, I would urge you to keep your eye on two specific points. First, you will see evidence that Trump's legal team, led by Rudy Giuliani, knew that they lacked actual evidence of widespread fraud sufficient to prove that the election was actually stolen.

"They knew it, but they went ahead with January 6th anyway. And second, consider how millions of Americans were persuaded to believe what Donald Trump's closest advisers in his administration did not. These Americans did not have access to the truth like Donald Trump did. They put their faith and their trust in Donald Trump.

"They wanted to believe in him. They wanted to fight for their country, and he deceived them. For millions of Americans, that may be painful to accept, but it is true. Thank you, Mr. Chairman. I yield back."

Bennie Thompson: "Without objection, the chair recognizes the gentlewoman from Florida, Ms. Murphy, and the gentleman from Maryland, Mr. Raskin, for opening statements."

Stephanie Murphy: "Thank you, Mr. Chairman. We know beyond a shadow of a doubt that then President Donald Trump lost in a free and fair election, and yet President Trump insisted that his loss was due to fraud in the election process rather than to the democratic will of the voters. The president continued to make this claim despite being told again and again by the courts, by the Justice Department, by his campaign officials, and by some of his closest advisers that the evidence did not support this assertion.

"This was the big lie, and millions of Americans were deceived by it. Too many of our fellow citizens still believe it to this day. It's corrosive to our country and damaging to our democracy. As our committee has shown in prior hearings, following the election, President Trump relentlessly pursued multiple interlocking lines of effort, all with a single goal, to remain in power despite having lost. The lines of effort were aimed at his loyal vice president, Mike Pence, at state election and elected officials, and at the US Department of Justice. The president pressured the vice president to obstruct the process to certify the election result. He demanded that state officials find him enough votes to overturn the election outcome in that state, and he pressed the Department of Justice to find widespread evidence of fraud.

"When Justice officials told the president that such evidence did not exist, the president urged them to simply declare that the election was corrupt. On December 14th, the Electoral College met to officially confirm that Joe Biden would be the next president. The evidence shows that once this occurred, President Trump and those who were willing to aid and abet him turned their attention to the joint session of Congress scheduled for January 6th at which the vice president would preside.

"In their warped view, this ceremonial event was the next and perhaps the last inflection point that could be used to reverse the outcome of the election before Mr. Biden's inauguration. As President Trump put it, the vice president and enough members of Congress simply needed to summon the courage to act.

"To help them find that courage, the president called for backup. Early in the morning of December 19th, the president sent out a tweet urging his followers to travel to Washington DC for January 6th. Be there, will be wild, the president wrote. As my colleague, Mr. Raskin, will describe in detail, this tweet served as a call to action and in some cases as a call to arms for many of President Trump's most loyal supporters.

"It's clear the president intended the assembled crowd on the — January 6th to serve his goal. And as you've already seen and as you will see again today, some of those who were coming had specific plans. The president's goal was to stay in power for a second term despite losing the election. The assembled crowd was one of the tools to achieve that goal.

"And in today's hearing, we will focus on events that took place in the final weeks leading up to January 6th, starting in mid-December, and we'll add color and context to evidence you've already heard about and will also provide additional new evidence. For example, you'll hear about meetings in which the president entertained extreme measures designed to help him stay in power like the seizure of voting machines.

"We will show some of the coordination that occurred between the White House and members of Congress as it relates to January 6th, and some of these members of Congress would later seek pardons. We will also examine some of the planning for the January 6th protests, placing special emphasis on one rally planner's concerns about the potential violence.

"And we will describe some of the president's key actions on the evening of January 5th and the morning of January 6th, including how the president edited and adlibbed his speech that morning at the Ellipse, directed the crowd to march to the Capitol, and spoke off script in a way that further inflamed an already angry crowd.

"I yield to the gentleman from Maryland, Mr. Raskin."

Jamie Raskin: "Thank you, Ms. Murphy, Mr. Chairman, Madam Vice Chair. Four days after the electors met across the country and made Joe Biden the president elect, Donald Trump was still trying to find a way to hang on to the presidency. On Friday, December 18th, his team of outside advisers paid him a surprise visit in the White House that would quickly become the stuff of legend.

"The meeting has been called unhinged, not normal and the craziest meeting of the Trump presidency. The outside lawyers who'd been involved in dozens of failed lawsuits had lots of theories supporting the big lie, but no evidence to support it. As we will see, however, they brought to the White House a draft executive order that they had prepared for President Trump to further his ends.

"Specifically, they proposed the immediate mass seizure of state election machines by the US military. The meeting ended after midnight with apparent rejection of that idea. In the wee hours of December 19th, dissatisfied with his options, Donald Trump decided to call for a large and wild crowd on Wednesday, January 6th, the day when Congress would meet to certify the electoral votes.

"Never before in American history had a president called for a crowd to come contest the counting of electoral votes by Congress or engaged in any effort designed to influence, delay, or obstruct the joint session of Congress in doing its work required by our Constitution and the Electoral Count Act. As we'll see, Donald Trump's 1:42 AM tweet electrified and galvanized his supporters, especially the dangerous extremists in the Oath Keepers, the Proud Boys, and other racist and white nationalist groups spoiling for a fight against the government.

"Three rings of interwoven attack were now operating towards January 6th. On the inside ring, Trump continued trying to work to overturn the election by getting Mike Pence to abandon his oath of office as vice president and assert the unilateral power to reject electoral votes. This would have been a fundamental and unprecedented breach of the Constitution that would promise Trump multiple ways of staying in office.

"Meanwhile, in the middle ring, members of domestic violent extremist groups created an alliance both online and in-person to coordinate a massive effort to storm, invade, and occupy the Capitol. By placing a target on the joint session of Congress, Trump had mobilized these groups around a common goal, emboldening them, strengthening their working relationships, and helping build their numbers.

"Finally, in the outer ring, on January 6th there assembled a large and angry crowd, the political force that Trump considered both the touchstone and the measure of his political power. Here were thousands of enraged Trump followers thoroughly convinced by the big lie, who traveled from across the country to join Trump's wild rally to stop the steal.

"With the proper incitement by political leaders and the proper instigation from the extremists, many members of this crowd could be led to storm the Capitol, confront the vice president and Congress, and try to overturn the 2020 election results. All of these efforts would converge and explode on January the 6th. Mr. Chairman, as you know better than any other member of this committee from the wrenching struggle for voting rights in your beloved Mississippi, the problem of politicians whipping up mob violence to destroy fair elections is the oldest domestic enemy of constitutional democracy in America.

"Abraham Lincoln knew it too. In 1837, a racist mob in Alton, Illinois broke into the offices of an abolitionist newspaper and killed its editor, Elijah Lovejoy. Lincoln wrote a speech in which he said that no transatlantic military giant could ever crush us as a nation, even with all of the fortunes in the world.

"But if downfall ever comes to America, he said, we ourselves would be its author and finisher. If racist mobs are encouraged by politicians to rampage and terrorize, Lincoln said, they will violate the rights of other citizens and quickly destroy the bonds of social trust necessary for democracy to work.

"Mobs and demagogues will put us on a path to political tyranny, Lincoln said. As we'll see today, this very old problem has returned with new ferocity today, as a president who lost an election deployed a mob, which included dangerous extremists, to attack the constitutional system of election and the peaceful transfer of power.

"And as we'll see, the creation of the Internet and social media has given today's tyrants tools of propaganda and disinformation that yesterday's despots could only have dreamed of. I yield back to the gentlelady from Florida, Ms. Murphy."

Stephanie Murphy: "Article Two of the United States Constitution establishes the Electoral College. Each state's laws provide that electors are to be chosen by a popular vote. And on December 14th, 2020, electors met in all 50 states and the District of Columbia to cast their votes. Joseph Biden won by a margin of 306 to 232. The election was over.

"Mr. Biden was the president elect. Before the Electoral College met, Donald Trump and his allies filed dozens of legal challenges to the election, but they lost over and over, again including in front of multiple judges — President Trump had nominated to the bench. In many of these cases, the judges were highly critical of the arguments put forward, explaining that no genuine evidence of widespread fraud had been presented. For example, a federal judge in Pennsylvania said, this court has been presented with strained legal arguments without merit and speculative accusations unsupported by evidence. In the United States of America, this cannot justify the disenfranchisement of a single voter, let alone all the voters of its six most populated states.

"On December 15th after the Electoral College certified the outcome, the Republican majority leader in the Senate acknowledged Mr. Biden's victory."

[multimedia]
Mitch McConnell: "Yesterday, electors met in all 50 states. So as of this morning, our country has officially a President-elect and a Vice President-elect. Many millions of us had hoped the Presidential election would yield a different result. But our system of government has processes to determine who will be sworn in on January the 20th. The Electoral College has spoken.

"So today, I want to congratulate President-elect Joe Biden."

Stephanie Murphy: "Even members of President Trump's Cabinet and his White House staff understood the significance of his losses in the courts and the absence of evidence of fraud. They also respected the constitutional certification by the Electoral College. Many of them told President Trump that it was time to concede the election to Mr. Biden.

"For example, then Secretary of Labor Gene Scalia, an accomplished lawyer and the son of late Justice Scalia called President Trump in mid-December and advised him to concede and accept the rulings of the courts."

Gene Scalia: "So I had to put a call into the President. I might have called on the 13th. We spoke, I believe, on the 14th in which I conveyed to him that I thought that it was time for him to acknowledge that President Biden had prevailed in the election. But I communicated to the President that when that legal process is exhausted and when the electors have voted, that that's the point at which that outcome needs to be expected.

"I told him that I did believe yes, that once those legal processes were run, if fraud had not been established that had affected the outcome of the election, then unfortunately, I believed that what had to be done was concede the outcome."

Stephanie Murphy: "As you've seen in prior hearings, President Trump's Justice Department, his White House staff, and his campaign officials were repeatedly telling him that there was no evidence of fraud sufficient to change the outcome of the election. And last week, we conducted an eight-hour interview with President Trump's White House Counsel, Pat Cipollone.

"You'll see a number of excerpts of that interview today and even more in our next hearing. Mr. Cipollone told us that he agreed with the testimony that there was no evidence of fraud sufficient to overturn the election."

[multimedia]
Unknown: "I want to start by asking if you agree, Mr. Cipollone, with the conclusion of Matt Morgan and Bill Barr, of all of the individuals who evaluated those claims that there is no evidence of election fraud sufficient

to undermine the outcome in any particular state?"

Pat Cipollone: "Yes, I agree with that."

Stephanie Murphy: "And Mr. Cipollone also specifically testified that he believed that Donald Trump should have conceded the election."

[multimedia]
Unknown: "Did you believe, Mr. Cipollone, that the President should concede once you made the determination based on the investigations that you credited — DOJ did. Did you in your mind form the belief that the President should concede the election loss at a certain point after the election."

Pat Cipollone: "Well, again, I was the White House counsel. Some of those decisions are political. So to the extent that — But — but if your question is did I believe he should concede the election at a point in time? Yes, I did. I believe Leader McConnell went on to the floor of the Senate, I believe in late December, and basically said, you know, the process is done.

"You know, that would be in line with my thinking on these things."

Stephanie Murphy: "As Attorney General Bill Barr testified, December 14 should have been the end of the matter."

[multimedia]
William Barr: "December 14th was the day that the states certified their votes and sent them to Congress. And in my view, that was

the end of the matter. I didn't see — you know, I thought that this would lead inexorably to a new administration."

Stephanie Murphy: "Mr. Cipollone also testified that the President's Chief of Staff Mark Meadows said he shared this view."

[multimedia]
Unknown: "As early as that November 23rd meeting, we understand that there was discussion about the President possibly conceding the election. And specifically, we understand that Mark

"Meadows assured both you and Attorney General Barr that the President would eventually agree to a graceful exit. Do you remember Mr. Meadows making any such representation?"

Pat Cipollone: "Are you saying as part of that meeting or separately? Again, without — without getting into that meeting, I would say that that is a — that is a statement and a sentiment that I heard from Mark Meadows."

Unknown: "I see. And again, do you know if it was on November 23rd or some point?"

Pat Cipollone: "Again, I — it was probably, you know, around that time and it was probably subsequent to that time. It wasn't a one-time statement."

Stephanie Murphy: "Mr. Meadows has refused to testify and the committee is in litigation with him. But many other White House officials shared the view that once the litigation ended and the Electoral College met, the election was over. And here is President Trump's former press secretary."

[multimedia]

Liz Cheney: "I wanted to clarify, Ms. McEnany. So back to my previous question. It was your view then — or was it your view that the efforts to overturn the election should have stopped once the litigation was complete?"

Kayleigh McEnany: "In my view, upon the conclusion of litigation was when I began to plan for life after the administration."

Stephanie Murphy: "And this is what Ivanka Trump told us."

[multimedia]

Unknown: "December 14th was the day on which the Electoral College met. When these electors around the country met and cast the electoral votes consistent with the — the popular vote in each state. And it was obviously a public proceeding or a series of proceedings that President Biden had obtained the requisite number of electors.

"Was that an important day for you? Did that affect sort of your planning or your realization as to whether or not there was going to be an end of this administration?"

Ivanka Trump: "I think so. I think it was my — my sentiment probably prior as well."

Stephanie Murphy: "Judd Deere was a White House deputy press secretary. This was his testimony about what he told President Trump."

[multimedia]

Judd Deere: "I told him that my personal viewpoint was that the Electoral College had met, which is the system that our country is — is set under to elect a President and Vice President. And I believed at that point that the means for him to pursue litigation was probably closed."

Unknown: "And do you recall what his response, if any, was?"

Judd Deere: "He disagreed."

Stephanie Murphy: "We've also seen this testimony from Attorney General Barr, reflecting a view of the White House staff in late November 2020."

[multimedia]

William Barr: "And then at that point I left. And as I walked out of the Oval Office, Jared was there with Dan Scavino who ran his — who ran the President's social media and who I thought was a reasonable guy, and believe is a reasonable guy. And I said how long is — how long is he going to carry on with this stolen election stuff?

"Where is this going to go? And by that time, Meadows had caught up with me and — leaving the office and caught up to me and said that — he said, look, I think that he's becoming more realistic and knows that there's a limit to how far he can take this. And then Jared said, you know, yeah, we're working on this.

"We're working on it."

Stephanie Murphy: "Likewise in this testimony. Cassidy Hutchinson, an aide to Mark Meadows, described her conversations with President Trump's Director of National Intelligence, John Ratcliffe, a former Republican Congressman."

[multimedia]
Cassidy Hutchinson: "He had expressed that he was concerned that it could spiral out of control and potentially be dangerous, either for our democracy or the way that things were going for the 6th."

Stephanie Murphy: "Of course, underlying all of this is the fundamental principle that the President of the United States cannot simply disregard the rulings of state and federal courts which are empowered to address specific election related claims. The President cannot simply pretend that the courts had not ruled."

[multimedia]
Liz Cheney: "By that time, the President or his associates had brought — had lost 60 out of 61 cases that they had brought to challenge different aspects of the election in a number of states. They lost 60 out of 61 of those cases. So by the time we get to January 3rd, that's — that's been clear. I assume, Pat, that you would agree the President is — is obligated to abide by the rulings of the courts."

Pat Cipollone: "Of course."

Liz Cheney: "And I assume you also –"

Pat Cipollone: "Everybody is obligated to abide by rules of courts."

Liz Cheney: "And I assume you also would agree the President has a particular obligation to take care that the laws be faithfully executed."

Pat Cipollone: "That is one of the President's obligations, correct."

Stephanie Murphy: "Yet President Trump disregarded these court rulings and the counsel from his closest advisors, and continued his efforts to cling to power. In our prior hearings, you have heard considerable testimony about President Trump's attempts to corruptly pressure Vice President Pence to refuse to count electoral votes, to corrupt the Department of Justice, to pressure state officials in state legislatures, and to create and submit a series of fake electoral slates.

"Now, we will show you what other actions President Trump was taking between December 14, 2020 and January 6th. I yield to the gentleman from Maryland, Mr. Raskin."

Jamie Raskin: "Thank you, Ms. Murphy. Throughout our hearings, you've heard how President Trump made baseless claims that voting machines were being manipulated by foreign powers in the 2020 election. You've also heard Trump's Attorney General Bill Barr describe such claims as complete nonsense, which he told the President.

"Let's review that testimony."

[multimedia]
William Barr: "I saw absolutely zero basis for the allegations, but they were made in such a sensational way that they obviously were influencing a lot of people, members of the public, that there was this systemic corruption

in the system and that their votes didn't count and that these machines controlled by somebody else were actually determining it, which was complete nonsense.

"And it was being laid out there, and I told them that it was — that it was crazy stuff and they were wasting their time on that. And it was doing a grave disservice to the country."

<u>Jamie Raskin</u>: "We've learned that President Trump's White House counsel agreed with the Department of Justice about this."

[multimedia]
<u>Unknown</u>: "Attorney General Barr made a public announcement on December 1st, less than a month after the election, that he had seen no systemic fraud [Inaudible]. Is it fair to say that by December 1st, you had reached the same conclusion?"

<u>Pat Cipollone</u>: "It's fair to say that I agreed with attorney general's — Attorney General Barr's conclusion on December 1st. Yes, I did. And I supported that conclusion."

<u>Jamie Raskin</u>: "However, the strong rejection of the attorney general and the White House counsel of these claims did not stop the President from trying to press them in public. But that's not all he did. Indeed, as you'll see in this clip, the President asked Attorney General Bill Barr to have the Department of Justice seize voting machines in the states."

[multimedia]
<u>William Barr</u>: "My recollection is the President said something like, well, we could get to the bottom — you know, some people

**say we could get to the bottom of this if — if
the department sees the machines. It was a
typical way of raising a point. And I said,
absolutely not. There's no probable cause and
I'm not going to seize any machines.**

"And that was that."

Unknown: "Yeah."

Jamie Raskin: "But this wasn't the end of the matter. On
the evening of December 18, 2020, Sidney Powell,
General Michael Flynn and others entered the White
House for an unplanned meeting with the President. The
meeting that would last multiple hours and become hot
blooded and contentious. The executive order behind me
on the screen was drafted on December the 16th, just two
days after the Electoral College vote by several of the
President's outside advisors over a luncheon at the Trump
International Hotel.

"As you can see here, this proposed order directs the
Secretary of Defense to seize voting machines, quote,
effective immediately. But it goes even further than that.
Under the order, President Trump would appoint a special
counsel with the power to seize machines and then charge
people with crimes with all resources necessary to carry
out her duties.

"The specific plan was to name Sidney Powell as special
counsel. The Trump lawyer who had spent the post-
election period making outlandish claims about
Venezuelan and Chinese interference in the election
among others. Here's what White House Counsel Pat
Cipollone had to say about Sidney Powell's qualifications
to take on such expansive authority."

[multimedia]

Pat Cipollone: "I don't think Sidney — Sidney Powell would say that I thought it was a good idea to appoint her special counsel. I was vehemently opposed. I didn't think she should have been appointed to anything."

Jamie Raskin: "Sidney Powell told the President that these steps were justified because of her evidence of foreign interference in the 2020 election.

"However, as we've seen, Trump's allies had no such evidence and of course no legal authority for the federal government to seize state voting machines. Here's Mr. Cipollone again denouncing Sidney Powell's terrible idea."

[multimedia]

Pat Cipollone: "There was a real question in my mind and a real concern, you know, particularly after the Attorney General had reached a conclusion that there wasn't sufficient election fraud to change the outcome of the election when other people kept suggesting that there was. The answer is, what is it? And at some point you have to put up or shut up. That was my view."

Unknown: "Why was this on a broader scale a bad idea for a country?"

Pat Cipollone: "To have the federal government seize voting machines? That's a terrible idea for the country. That's not how we do things in the United States. There's no legal authority to do that. And there is a way to contest elections. You know, that — that happens all the time. But the idea that the federal government could come in and seize election machines, no. That — that's — I don't

— I don't understand why we even have to tell you why that's a bad idea for the country.

"It's a terrible idea."

Jamie Raskin: "For all of it's absurdity, the December 18th meeting was critically important because President Trump got to watch up close for several hours as his White House counsel and other White House lawyers destroyed the baseless factual claims and ridiculous legal arguments being offered by Sidney Powell, Mike Flynn, and others.

"President Trump now knew all of these claims were nonsense, not just from his able White House lawyers but also from his own Department of Justice officials and indeed his own campaign officials. As White House counsel Pat Cipollone told us."

[multimedia]
Pat Cipollone: "With respect to the whole election fraud issue, it to me is sort of if you're going to make those kind of claims — and people were open to them early on because people were making all sorts of claims. And the real question is show the evidence. Ok?"

Jamie Raskin: "It wasn't just the Justice Department, the Trump campaign, and the Trump White House lawyers who knew it. Even Rudy Giuliani's own legal team admitted that they did not have any real evidence of fraud sufficient to change the election result. Here's an e-mail from Rudy Giuliani's lead investigator, Bernie Kerik.

"On December 28th, 2022 to Chief of Staff Mark Meadows. Mr. Kerik did not mince any words. 'We can do all the investigations we want later. But if the President plans on winning, it's the legislators that have to be moved and this will do just that.' Mr. Kerik wanted the President to win. What he didn't say in this email was what he would later tell the select committee in a letter that his lawyer wrote to us in November.

"The letter said quote, 'It was impossible for Mr. Kerik and his team to determine conclusively whether there was widespread fraud or whether that widespread fraud would have altered the outcome of the election.' In other words, even Rudy Giuliani's own legal team knew before January 6th that they hadn't collected enough actual evidence to support any of their stolen election claims.

"Here's what Trump campaign senior adviser Jason Miller told the committee about some of the so-called evidence of fraud that the campaign had seen from the Giuliani team."

> [multimedia]
> **Unknown: "So do you know what the examples of fraud — numbers, names, and supporting evidence — was that you sent to Mo Brooks' office. And I say you, I mean you or the campaign."**
>
> **Jason Miller: "There are some very, very general documents as far as — as far as, say, for example, here are the handful of dead people in several different states. Here are explanations on a couple of the legal challenges as far as the saying that the — the rules were changed an unconstitutional manner. But it was — to say that it was spin is — is probably an understatement."**

Jamie Raskin: "Here's how President Trump's deputy campaign manager described the evidence of fraud that the campaign had seen."

> [multimedia]
> **Unknown: "You never came to learn or understand that Mayor Giuliani had — had**

produced evidence of election fraud. Is that
fair?"

Justin Clark: "That's fair."

Jamie Raskin: "And here's testimony that we received
from the speaker of the Arizona House of Representatives,
Rusty Bowers, about an exchange that he had with Rudy
Giuliani after the election."

[multimedia]
Adam Schiff: "At some point, did one of them
make a comment that they didn't have
evidence but they had a lot of theories?"

Rusty Bowers: "That was Mr. Giuliani."

Jamie Raskin: "Chief of Staff Mark Meadows told people
that he thought Trump should concede around the time the
Electoral College certified the result. But nonetheless he
later worked to try to facilitate President Trump's wishes.
Here's what Cassidy Hutchinson told us."

[multimedia]
Cassidy Hutchinson: "During this period, he
— I perceived his goal with all of this to keep
Trump in office. You know, he had very
seriously and deeply considered the allegations
of voter fraud. But when he began
acknowledging that maybe there wasn't
enough voter fraud to overturn the election,
you know, I — I witnessed him start to explore
potential constitutional loopholes more
extensively, which I then connected with John
Eastman's theories."

Jamie Raskin: "The startling conclusion is this: even an
agreed upon complete lack of evidence could not stop
President Trump, Mark Meadows, and their allies from

trying to overturn the results of a free and fair election. So let's return to that meeting at the White House on the evening of December 18. That night, a group showed up at the White House including Sidney Powell, retired Lieutenant General Michael Flynn, and former Overstock.com CEO Patrick Byrne.

"After gaining access to the building from a junior White House staffer, the group made their way to the Oval Office. They were able to speak with the President by himself for some time until White House officials learned of the meeting. What ensued was a heated and profane clash between this group and President Trump's White House advisors who traded personal insults, accusations of disloyalty to the President, and even challenges to physically fight.

"The meeting would last over six hours, beginning here in the Oval Office, moving around the West Wing, and many hours later ending up in the President's private residence. The select committee has spoken with six of the participants as well as staffers who could hear the screaming from outside the Oval Office. What took place next is best told in their own words as you will see from this video."

> **[multimedia]**
> **Unknown: "Did you believe that it was going to work, that you were going be able to get to see the President without an appointment?"**
>
> **Sidney Powell: "I had no idea."**
>
> **Unknown: "In fact you do get to see the President without an appointment."**
>
> **Sidney Powell: "We did."**

Unknown: "How much time did you have alone with the President? I say alone, you had other people with you, but, I think from his aides before the crowd came running."

Sidney Powell: "Probably no more than 10 or 15 minutes."

Unknown: "Was in that –"

Sidney Powell: "— I bet Pat Cipollone set a new land speed record."

Pat Cipollone: "I got a call either for Molly or from Eric Herschmann that I need to get to the Oval Office."

Cassidy Hutchinson: "So that was the first point that I had recognized, Ok, there is nobody in there from the White House. Mark's gone. What's going on right now."

Pat Cipollone: "I opened the door and I walked in, I saw General Flynn, I saw Sidney Powell sitting there. I was not happy to see the people who were in the Oval Office."

Unknown: "Explain why."

Pat Cipollone: "Well, again, I — I don't think they were providing — well, first of all, the Overstock person I - - I've never met — never. I never knew who this guy was. Actually the first thing I did, I walked in, I looked at him, and I said who are you? And he told me. I don't think — I don't think any of these people were providing the President with good advice.

"And so I — I — I didn't understand how they had gotten in."

Unknown: "In the short period of time that you had with the President, did he seem receptive to the presentation that you were making?"

Sidney Powell: "He was very interested in hearing particularly about the CISA findings and the terms of 13848 that apparently nobody else had bothered to inform him of."

Eric Herschmann: "And I was asking, like, are you're claiming the Democrats were working with Hugo Chavez, Venezuelans, and whomever else. And at one point General Flynn took out a diagram that supposedly showed IP addresses all over the world. And — or ISP — who was — who was communicating with whom via the machines and some comment about like Nest thermostats being hooked up to the Internet."

Unknown: "So it's been reported that during this meeting, Ms. Powell talked about Dominion voting machines and made various election fraud claims that involve foreign countries such as Venezuela, Iran, and China. Is that accurate?"

Michael Flynn: "The fifth."

Unknown: "Was the meeting tense?"

Derek Lyons: "Oh yeah. I — it was not a casual meeting."

Unknown: "Explain."

Derek Lyons: "I mean, at times there were people shouting at each other, hurling insults at each other. It wasn't just sort of people sitting around on the couch like chit chatting."

Unknown: "Do you recall whether he raised to Ms. Powell the fact that she and the campaign had lost all of the 60 cases that they had brought in litigation?"

Pat Cipollone: "Yes. He raised that."

Unknown: "And what was the response?"

Pat Cipollone: "I don't remember what she said. I don't think it was a good response."

Sidney Powell: "Cipollone and Herschmann and whoever the other guy was showed nothing but contempt and disdain of the President."

Pat Cipollone: "I remember the three of them were really sort of forcefully attacking me verbally. Eric, Derek, and we were pushing back and we were asking one simple question as a — as a general matter. Where is the evidence? So."

Unknown: "What response did you get when you asked Ms. Powell and her colleagues where's the evidence?"

Pat Cipollone: "A variety of responses based on my current recollection including, you know, I can't believe you would say something, like, you know, things like this. Like, 'What do you mean where's the evidence? You should know.' Yeah, I — things like that or, you know, a disregard, I would say, a general disregard for the importance of actually backing up what you say with facts."

Derek Lyons: "And, you know, then there was discussion of, well, you know, we don't have it now but we will have it or whatever."

Sidney Powell: "I mean, if — if it had been me sitting in his chair, I would have fired all of them that night and had em escorted out of the building."

Eric Herschmann: "Which Derek and I both challenged what she was saying. And she says, well, the judges are corrupt. And I was like, every one? Every single case that you've done in the country you guys lost, every one of them is corrupt? Even the ones we appointed? And I'm being nice. I was much more harsh to her."

Unknown: "So one of the other things that's been reported that was said during this meeting was that President Trump told White House lawyers Mr. Herschmann and Mr. Cipollone that they weren't offering him any solutions, but Ms. Powell and others were. So why not try what Ms. Powell and others were proposing? Do you remember anything along those lines being said by President Trump?"

Derek Lyons: "I do. That sounds right."

Eric Herschmann: "I think that it got to the point where the screaming was completely, completely out there. I mean, you got people walk in, it was late at night, had been a long day. And what they were proposing I thought was nuts."

Rudy Giuliani: "I'm gonna — I'm gonna categorically describe it as you guys are not tough enough. Or maybe I put it another way. You're a bunch of pussies. Excuse the expression, but that — that's I — I'm almost certain the word was used."

Eric Herschmann: "Flynn screamed at me that I was a quitter and everything, kept on standing up and turning around and screaming at me. And a certain point I had it with him. So I yelled back better come over. Better sit your effing ass back down."

Rudy Giuliani: "The President and the White House team went upstairs to the residence, but to the public part of the residence. You know, the big — the big parlor where you can have meetings in the conference room."

Unknown: "Yellow oval. They call that the yellow level."

Rudy Giuliani: "Yes, exactly. The yellow oval office. I always called it the upper. And I'm not exactly sure where the Sidney group went. I think maybe the Roosevelt Room. And I stayed — In the Cabinet Room, which is kind of cool. I really liked that, all my — all by myself."

Unknown: "At the end of the day, we landed where we started the meeting, at least from a structural standpoint, which was Sidney Powell was fighting. Mike Flynn was fighting. They were looking for avenues that would enable — that would result in President

Trump remaining President Trump for a second term."

<u>Jamie Raskin</u>: "The meeting finally ended after midnight. Here are text messages sent by Cassidy Hutchinson during and after the meeting. As you can see, Ms. Hutchinson reported that the meeting in the West Wing was unhinged. The meeting finally broke up after midnight. During the early morning of December 19, Cassidy Hutchinson captured the moment of Mark Meadows escorting Rudy Giuliani off the White House grounds to 'make sure he didn't wander back into the mansion.' Certain accounts of this meeting indicate that President Trump actually granted Ms. Powell security clearance and appointed her to a somewhat ill defined position of special counsel."

<u>Sidney Powell</u>: "He asked Pat Cipollone if he had the authority to name a special counsel, and he said yes. And then he asked him if he had the authority to give me whatever security clearance I needed, and Pat Cipollone said yes. And then the president said, Ok, you know, I'm the naming her that and I'm giving her security clearance.

"And then shortly before we left and it totally blew up, that's when Cipollone and/or Herschmann and whoever the other young man was said you can name her whatever you want to name her, and no one's going to pay any attention to it."

<u>Unknown</u>: "How did he respond? How did the president respond to that?"

Sidney Powell: "Something like you see what I deal with. I deal with this all the time."

Jamie Raskin: "Over the ensuing days, no further steps were taken to appoint Sidney Powell, but there is some ambiguity about what the president actually said and did during the meeting. Here is how Pat Cipollone described it."

[multimedia]

Pat Cipollone: "I don't know what her understanding of whether she had been appointed, what she had been appointed to, Ok? In my view, she hadn't been appointed to anything and ultimately wasn't appointed to anything, because there had to be other steps taken. And that was my view when I left the meeting. But she may have a different view, and others may have a different view, and — and the president may have a different view."

Liz Cheney: "Were any steps taken, including the president himself telling her she'd been appointed?"

Pat Cipollone: "Again, I'm not going to get into what the president said in the meeting. You know, my recollection is you're not appointed even — you're not appointed until — until steps are taken to get the paperwork done, get — and when I left the meeting, Ok — I guess — I guess what I'm trying to say is I'm not going to get into what the president said or want — said he wanted."

Jamie Raskin: "Mr. Cipollone, when the matter continued to flare up over the next several days, was it your understanding that Sidney Powell was still seeking an appointment or that she was asserting that she had been appointed by the president at the December 18 meeting?"

Pat Cipollone: "You know, now that you mention it, probably both, you know, in — in terms of like I think she was — I think she may have been of the view that she had been appointed and was seeking to, you know, get — get that done, and — and — and that she should be appointed."

Jamie Raskin: "As you listen to these clips, remember that Ms. Powell, the person who President Trump tried to make special counsel, was ultimately sanctioned by a federal court and sued by Dominion Voting Systems for defamation. In her own defense to that lawsuit, Sidney Power argued that 'no reasonable person would conclude that the statements were truly statements of fact.' Not long after Sidney Powell, General Flynn, and Rudy Giuliani — Giuliani left the White House in the early hours of the morning, President Trump turned away from both his outside advisers' most outlandish and unworkable schemes and his White House counsel's advice to swallow hard and accept the reality of his loss.

"Instead, Donald Trump issued a tweet that would galvanize his followers, unleash a political firestorm, and change the course of our history as a country. Trump's purpose was to mobilize a crowd. And how do you mobilize a crowd in 2020? With millions of followers on Twitter, President Trump knew exactly how to do it. At 1:42 AM on December 19, 2020, shortly after the last participants left the unhinged meeting, Trump sent out the tweet with his explosive invitation.

"Trump repeated his big lie and claimed it was 'statistically impossible to have lost the 2020 election' before calling for a big protest in DC on January 6th, be there, will be wild. Trump supporters responded immediately. Women for America First, a pro-Trump organizing group, had previously applied for a rally permit for January 22nd and 23rd in Washington, DC, several days after Joe Biden was to be inaugurated.

"But in the hours after the tweet, they moved their permit to January 6th, two weeks before. This rescheduling created the rally where Trump would eventually speak. The next day, Ali Alexander, leader of the Stop the Steal organization and a key mobilizer of Trump supporters, registered Wildprotest.com, named after Trump's tweet.

"Wildprotest.com provided comprehensive information about numerous newly organized protest events in Washington. It included event times, places, speakers, and details on transportation to Washington DC. Meanwhile, other key Trump supporters, including far right media personalities, began promoting the wild protest on January 6th."

[multimedia]
Alex Jones: "It's Saturday, December 19th. The year is 2020, and one of the most historic events in American history has just taken place. President Trump, in the early morning hours today, tweeted that he wants the American people to march on Washington DC on January 6th, 2021."

Tim Pool: "And now Donald Trump is calling on his supporters to descend on Washington DC January 6th."

Alex Jones: "He is now calling on we the People to take action and to show our numbers."

Matt Bracken: "We're going to only be saved by millions of Americans moving to Washington, occupying the entire area, if — if necessary storming right into the Capitol. You know, they're — we know the rules of engagement. If you have enough people, you can push down any kind of a fence or a wall."

Tim Pool: "This could be Trump's last stand. And it's a time when he has specifically called on his supporters to arrive in DC. That's something that may actually be the big push Trump supporters need to say this is it. It's now or never."

Salty Cracker: "Ya better understand something, son. Ya better understand something. Red wave, bitch. Red wed — there's gonna be a red wedding going down January 6th."

Tim Pool: "On that day, Trump says show up for a protest. It's gonna be wild. And based on what we've already seen from the previous events, I think Trump is absolutely correct."

Salty Cracker: "Motherfucker, you better look outside. You better look out January 6th. Kick that fucking door open, look down the street. There're gonna be a million plus geeked up armed Americans."

Alex Jones: "The time for games is over. The time for action is now. Where were you when history called? Where were you when you and your children's destiny and future was on the line?"

Jamie Raskin: "In that clip, you heard one of Trump's supporters predict a red wedding, which is a pop culture reference to mass slaughter. But the point is that Trump's call to Washington reverberated powerfully and pervasively online. The committee has interviewed a former Twitter employee, who explained the effect that Trump had on the Twitter platform.

"This employee was on the team responsible for platform and content moderation policies on Twitter throughout 2020 and 2021. The employee testified that Twitter considered adopting a stricter content moderation policy after President Trump told the Proud Boys to stand back and stand by from the lectern at the September 29th presidential debate, but Twitter chose not to act.

"Here's the former employee, whose voice has been obscured to protect their identity, discussing Trump's stand back and stand by comment and the effect it had."

[multimedia]

Unknown: "My concern was that the former president, for seemingly the first time, was speaking directly to extremist organizations and giving them directives. We had not seen that sort of direct communication before, and that concerned me. So, just to clarify further, you were worried, others at Twitter were worried, that the president might use your platform to speak directly to folks who might be incited to violence?

"Yes. I believe that Twitter relished in the knowledge that they were also the favorite and most used service of the former president, and enjoyed having that sort of power within the social media ecosystem. If President Trump were anyone else, would it have taken until January 2021 for him to be suspended?

"Absolutely not. If Donald — if former President Donald Trump were any other user on Twitter, he would have been permanently suspended a very long time ago."

Jamie Raskin: "Despite these grave concerns, Trump remained on the platform completely unchecked. Then came the December 19 tweet, and everything it inspired. Indeed —"

[multimedia]
Unknown: "It was — it felt as if — if a mob was being organized, and they were gathering together their weaponry and their logic and their reasoning behind why they were prepared to fight. Prior to December 19th, again, it was — it was vague. It was — it was nonspecific but very clear that individuals were ready, willing, and able to take up arms.

"After this tweet on December 19th, again, it became clear not only were these individuals ready and willing, but the leader of their cause was asking them to join him in this cause and in fighting for this cause in DC on January 6th as well. I will also say what shocked me was the responses to these tweets, right?

"So, these were — a lot of the locked and loaded, stand back, stand by, those tweets were in response to Donald Trump saying things like this, right? So, there would be a response that said big protest in DC on January 6th, be there, be wild, and someone would respond and say I'm locked and loaded and ready for civil war part two, right?

"I very much believe that Donald Trump posting this tweet on December 19th was essentially staking flag in DC on January 6th for his supporters to come and rally. And you were concerned about the potential for this gathering becoming violent? Absolutely."

Jamie Raskin: "Indeed, many of Trump's followers took to social media to declare that they were ready to answer Trump's call. One user asked is the 6th D-Day? Is that why Trump wants everyone there? Another asserted Trump just told us all to come armed. Fucking A, this is happening. A third took it even further. It will be wild means we need volunteers for the firing squad.

"Jim Watkins, the owner of 8kun, the fringe online forum that was birthplace of the QAnon extremist movement, confirmed the importance of Trump's tweet."

[multimedia]
Unknown: "Why did you first decide to go to DC for January 6th?"

Jim Watkins: "When — when the president of the United States announced that he was going to have a rally, then I bought ticket went."

Jamie Raskin: "Watkins was at the Capitol on January 6th. Some who have since been indicted for their involvement in the attack on the Capitol also responded. One of them posted on the 19th, 'Calling all patriots. Be in Washington DC January the 6th. This wasn't organized by any group. DJT has invited us, and it's going to be wild.' Some of the online rhetoric turned openly homicidal and white nationalist, such as why don't we just kill them, every last Democrat, down to the last man, woman, and child, and it's time for the day of the rope.

"White revolution is the only solution. Others realized that police would be standing in the way of their effort to overturn the election, so one wrote I'm ready to die for my beliefs. Are you ready to die, police? Another wrote on thedonald.win, cops don't have standing if they're laying on the ground in a pool of their own blood.

"Thedonald.win was an openly racist and anti-Semitic forum. The Select Committee deposed that site's founder, Jody Williams. He confirmed how the president's tweet created a laser like focus on the date of January the 6th."

> **[multimedia]**
> **Jody Williams**: "And people had been talking about going to DC since the election was over."
>
> **Unknown**: "And do you recall whether or not the conversation around those dates centered on the 6th after the president's tweet?"
>
> **Jody Williams**: "Oh, sure. Yeah. I mean after it was announced that, you know, he was going to be there on the 6th to talk, yes. Then — then anything else was kind of shut out and it was just gonna on the sixth."
>
> **Unknown**: "Ok. And that was pretty clearly reflected in the — the content on — on the site?"
>
> **Jody Williams**: "Yeah. Yeah, sure."

Jamie Raskin: "On that site, many shared plans and violent threats. Bring handcuffs and wait near the tunnels, wrote one user. A commenter replied suggesting zip ties instead. One post encouraged others to come with body armor, knuckles, shields, bats, pepper spray, whatever it takes. All of those were used on the 6th. The post concluded, join your local Proud Boys chapter as well.

"Thedonald.win featured discussions of the tunnels beneath the Capitol complex, suggestions for targeting members of Congress, and encouragement to attend this once in a lifetime event. While Trump supporters grew more aggressive online, he continued to rile up his base on Twitter. He said there was overwhelming evidence that the election was the biggest scam in our nation's history.

"As you can see, the president continued to boost the event, tweeting about it more than a dozen times in the lead up to January the 6th. Mr. Chairman, I reserve."

Bennie Thompson: "The chair requests that those in a hearing room remain seated until the Capitol Police have escorted members from the room. Pursuant to the order of the committee of today, the chair declares the committee in recess for a period of approximately 10 minutes. Committee will be in order. Chair recognizes gentleman from Maryland, Mr. Raskin."

Jamie Raskin: "Mr. Chairman, President Trump's tweet drew tens of thousands of Americans to Washington to form the angry crowd that would be transformed on January the sixth into a violent mob. Dr. Donell Harvin, who is the chief of Homeland Security and intelligence for DC, told the committee how his team saw Trump's December 19th tweet unite violent groups across the spectrum on the far right."

> **[multimedia]**
> **Donell Harvin: "We — we got derogatory information from OSINT suggesting that some very, very violent individuals were organizing to come to DC, and not only were they organized to come to DC, but they were — these groups, these nonaligned groups were aligning. And so the rent - - all the red flags went up at that point.**

"You know, when you have armed militia collaborating with white supremacy groups collaborating with conspiracy theory groups online all toward a common goal, you start seeing what we call in, you know, terrorism, a blended ideology. And that's a very, very bad sign. Then when they were clearly across — not just across one platform, but across multiple platforms of these groups coordinating, not just like chatting, hey, how's it going?

"You know what's the weather like where you're at? But like, what are you bringing? What are you wearing? You know, where — where — where do we meet up? Do you have plans for the Capitol? That operational — that's like pre operational intelligence, right? And that — that is something that's clearly alarming."

<u>Jamie Raskin</u>: "The Proud Boys and the Oath Keepers are two key groups that responded immediately to President Trump's call. The Proud Boys are a far right street fighting group that glorifies violence and white supremacy. The Oath Keepers are extremists who promote a wide range of conspiracy theories and sought to act as a private paramilitary force for Donald Trump.

"The Department of Justice has charged leaders of both groups with seditious conspiracy to overthrow the government of the United States on January the sixth. Trump's December 19th tweet motivated these two extremist groups, which have historically not worked together to coordinate their activities. On December 19th at 10:22 a.m., just hours after President Trump's tweet, Kelly Meggs, the head of the Florida Oath Keepers, declared an alliance among the Oath Keepers, the Proud

Boys and the Florida Three Percenters, another militia group.

"He wrote, we have decided to work together and shut this shit down. Phone records obtained by the Select Committee show that later that afternoon, Mr. Meggs called Proud Boys leader Enrique Tarrio, and they spoke for several minutes. The very next day, the Proud Boys got to work. The Proud Boys launched an encrypted chat called the Ministry of Self-defense.

"The committee obtained hundreds of these messages, which show strategic and tactical planning about January the 6th, including maps of Washington, DC that pinpoint the location of police. In the weeks leading up to the attack, leaders in both the Proud Boys and the Oath Keepers worked with Trump allies. One such ally was Lieutenant General Michael Flynn, Trump's former national security advisor and one of the participants in the unhinged meeting at the White House on December 18th. He also had connections to the Oath Keepers.

"This photo from December 12th shows Flynn and Patrick Byrne, another Trump ally, who was present at that December 18th meeting guarded by indicted Oath Keeper Roberto Minuta. Another view of the scene shows Oath Keepers leader Stewart Rhodes in the picture as well. Another central figure with ties to this network of extremist groups was Roger Stone, a political consultant and longtime confidant of President Trump.

"He pardoned both Flynn and Stone in the weeks between the election on November 3rd and January 6th. In the same time frame, Stone communicated with both the Proud Boys and the Oath Keepers regularly. The committee obtained encrypted content from a group - - from a group chat called Friends of Stone, FOS, which included Stone, Rhodes, Tarrio and Ali Alexander.

"The chat focused on various pro-Trump events in November and December of 2020, as well as January 6th. As you can see here, Stewart Rhodes himself urged the Friends of Stone to have people go to their state capitols if they could not make it to Washington for the first million MAGA March on November 14th. These friends of Roger Stone had a significant presence at multiple pro-Trump events after the election, including in Washington on December the 12th. On that day, Stewart Rhodes called for Donald Trump to invoke martial law, promising bloodshed if he did not."

> **[multimedia]**
> **Unknown: "We need to know from you that you are with him, that he does not do it now while he is commander in chief, we're going to have to do it ourselves later in a much more desperate, much more bloody war. Let's get it on now while he is still the commander in chief. Hooah."**

Jamie Raskin: "That night, the Proud Boys engaged in violence on the streets of Washington and hurled aggressive insults at the police."

> **[multimedia]**
> **Unknown: "You oath breakers, do your fucking job. Give us one hour, one hour."**

Jamie Raskin: "Just the previous night, the co-host of Infowars issued an ominous warning at a rally alongside Roger Stone and Proud Boys leader Enrique Tarrio."

> **[multimedia]**
> **Unknown: "[Inaudible] We will be back in January."**

Jamie Raskin: "Encrypted chats obtained by the Select Committee show that Kelly Meggs, the indicted leader of the Florida Oath Keepers, spoke directly with Roger Stone about security on January 5th and 6th. In fact, on January 6th, Stone was guarded by two Oath Keepers who have since been criminally indicted for seditious conspiracy.

"One of them later pleaded guilty and, according to the Department of Justice, admitted that the Oath Keepers were ready to use, quote, lethal force if necessary against anyone who tried to remove President Trump from the White House, including the National Guard. As we've seen, the Proud Boys were also part of the Friends of Stone Network.

Stone's ties to the Proud Boys go back many years. He's even taken their so-called fraternity creed required for the first level of initiation to the group."

> [multimedia]
> **Roger Stone**: "Hi, I'm Roger Stone. I'm a **Western chauvinist, and I refuse to apologize for creating the modern world.**"

> **Unknown**: "Thank you, Roger."

Jamie Raskin: "Kelly Sorrell, a lawyer who assists the Oath Keepers and a volunteer lawyer for the Trump campaign, explained to the committee how Roger Stone and other figures brought extremists of different stripes and views together."

> [multimedia]
> **Unknown**: "You mentioned that Mr. Stone wanted to start the Stop the Steal series of rallies. Who did you consider the leader of these rallies? It sounds like from what you just said, it was Mr. Stone, Mr. Jones, and Mr. Ali Alexander. Is that correct?"

Kelly Sorrell: "Those are the ones that became like the — the center point for everything."

Jamie Raskin: "We'll learn more from Ms. Murphy about these individuals and their involvement in the days leading up to the violent attack on January 6th. We'll also hear how they were allowed to speak at a rally for President Trump the night before January 6th, even though organizers had expressed serious concerns about their violent and extremist rhetoric directly to Mark Meadows.

"And you'll hear testimony from White House aides who were with the President as he watched the crowd from the Oval Office, and will testify about how excited he was for the following day. Let me note now that our investigation continues on these critical issues. We have only shown a small fraction of what we have found.

"I look forward to the public release of more of our findings later, Mr. Chairman, and I now yield back."

Bennie Thompson: The gentleman yields back. The Chair recognizes the gentlewoman from Florida, Ms. Murphy.

Stephanie Murphy: "During our most recent hearing, the committee showed some evidence of what President Trump, Chief of Staff Mark Meadows, and other White House officials knew about the potential for violence on January 6th. And despite this information, they made no effort to cancel the rally, halt the march to the Capitol, or even to lower the temperature among President Trump's supporters.

"Katrina Pierson, one of the organizers of January 6th rally and a former campaign spokeswoman for President Trump, grew increasingly apprehensive after learning that multiple activists had been proposed as speakers for the January 6th rally. These included some of the people we discussed earlier in this hearing.

"Roger Stone, a longtime outside advisor to President Trump; Alex Jones, the founder of the conspiracy theory website Infowars; and Ali Alexander, an activist known for his violent political rhetoric. On December 30th, Miss Pierson exchanged text messages with another key rally organizer about why people like Mr. Alexander and Mr. Jones were being suggested as speakers at the President's rally on January 6th. Ms. Pierson's explanation was POTUS, and she remarks that the President likes the crazies.

"The committee asked Ms. Pierson about these messages and this is what she said."

> **[multimedia]**
> **Unknown:** "So when you said that he likes the crazies, were you talking about President Trump?"
>
> **Katrina Pierson:** "Yes, I was talking about President Trump. He loved people who viciously defended him in public."
>
> **Unknown:** "But consistent, in terms of the support for these people, at least with what the President likes from what you could tell."
>
> **Katrina Pierson:** "Yes, these are people that would be very, very vicious in publicly defending him."

Stephanie Murphy: "On January 2nd, Ms. Pierson's concerns about the potential rally speakers had grown serious enough that she reached out to Mr. Meadows directly. She wrote, Good afternoon. Would you mind giving me a call regarding this January 6 event? Things have gotten crazy and I desperately need some direction, please.

"Please According to phone records obtained by the committee. Ms. Pierson received a phone call from Mr. Meadows 8 minutes later. Here is what Ms. Pierson said about that conversation."

[multimedia]
Unknown: "So what specifically did you tell them, though, about other — other events?"

Katrina Pierson: "Just that there were a bunch of entities coming in. Some were very suspect, but they're going to be on other — on other stages, some on other days. A very, very brief overview of what was actually happening and why I raised the red flags."

Unknown: "And when you told him that people were very suspect, what — what — did you tell him what you meant by that? Or what did you convey to him about what — the problems with these folks?"

Katrina Pierson: "I think I even texted him some of my concerns, but I did briefly go over some of the concerns that I had raised to everybody with Alex Jones or Ali Alexander and some of the rhetoric that they were doing. I probably mentioned to him that they had already caused trouble at other capitols — or at the previous event, the previous march that they did for protesting.

"And I just had a concern about it."

Stephanie Murphy: "Ms. Pierson was especially concerned about Ali Alexander and Alex Jones, because in November 2020, both men and some of their supporters had entered the Georgia State Capitol to protest the results of the 2020 election. Ms. Pierson believed that she mentioned this to Mark Meadows on this January 2nd call.

"Notably, January 2nd is the same day on which, according to Cassidy Hutchinson. Ms. Meadows — Mr. Meadows warned her of things — that things might get real, real bad on January 6. After her January 2nd call with Mr. Meadows, Katrina Pierson sent an email to fellow rally organizers. She wrote, POTUS expectations are to have something intimate at the Ellipse, and call on everyone to march to the Capitol.

"The President's own documents suggest that the President had decided to call on his supporters to go to the Capitol on January 6, but that he chose not to widely announce it until his speech on the Ellipse that morning. The committee has obtained this draft, updated — undated tweet from the National Archives.

"It includes a stamp stating, President has seen. The draft tweet reads: I will be making a big speech at 10 a.m. on January 6 at the Ellipse south of the White House. Please arrive early. Massive crowds expected. March to the Capitol after. Stop the steal. Although this tweet was never sent, rally organizers were discussing and preparing for the march to the Capitol in the days leading up to January 6. This is a January 4th text message from a rally organizer to Mike Lindell, the MyPillow CEO. The organizer says, you know, this stays between us. We're having a second stage at the Supreme Court again, after the Ellipse.

"POTUS is going to have us march there/the Capitol. It cannot get out about the second stage, because people will try and set up another and sabotage it. It can also not get out about the march, because I will be in trouble with the National Park Service and all the agencies. But POTUS is going to just call for it, quote, unexpectedly.

"The end of the message indicates that the President's plan to have his followers march to the Capitol was not being broadly discussed. And then on the morning of January 5th, Ali Alexander, whose firebrand style concerned Katrina Pierson, sent a similar text to a conservative journalist. Mr. Alexander said, Tomorrow: Ellipse, then US Capitol.

"Trump is supposed to order us to the Capitol at the end of his speech, but we will see. President Trump did follow through on his plan using his January 6th speech to tell his supporters to march to the Capitol on January 6. The evidence confirms that this was not a spontaneous call to action, but rather was a deliberate strategy decided upon in advance by the President.

"Another part of the President's strategy involves certain members of Congress who amplified his unsupported assertions that the election had been stolen. In the weeks after the election, the White House coordinated closely with President Trump's allies in Congress to disseminate his false claims and to encourage members of the public to fight the outcome on January 6. We know that the President met with various members to discuss January 6 well before the joint session.

"The President's private schedule for December 21, 2020, shows a private meeting with Republican members of Congress. We know that Vice President Pence, Chief of Staff Mark Meadows, and Rudy Giuliani also attended that meeting. We obtained an email that was sent from Congressman Mo Brooks of Alabama to Mark Meadows, setting up that meeting.

"The subject line is: White House meeting December 21st regarding January 6. In his email, Congressman Brooks explained that he had not asked anyone to join him in the, quote, January 6 effort because in his view, quote, only citizens can exert the necessary influence on Senators and

Congressmen to join this fight against massive voter fraud and election theft. At this point, you may also recall testimony given in our earlier hearing by Acting Attorney General Richard Donoghue who said that the President asked the Department of Justice to, quote, just say that the election was corrupt and leave the rest to me and the Republican Congressman. According to White House visitor logs obtained by the committee, members of Congress present at the White House on December 21st included Congressman Brian Babin, Andy Biggs, Matt Gaetz, Louie Gohmert, Paul Gosar, Andy Harris, Jody Hice, Jim Jordan, and Scott Perry.

"Then Congresswoman-elect Marjorie Taylor Greene was also there. We heard testimony in an earlier hearing that a pardon was ultimately requested by Congressman Mo Brooks and other members of Congress Congress who attended this meeting. We've asked witnesses what happened during the December 21st meeting, and we've learned that part of the discussion centered on the role of the vice president during the counting of the electoral votes.

"These members of Congress were discussing what would later be known as the Eastman theory, which was being pushed by attorney John Eastman. In one of our earlier hearings, you heard in great detail that President Trump was trying to convince Vice President Pence to do something illegal. His White House counsel confirmed all of that in testimony last week."

[multimedia]
Unknown: "Your view, Mr. Cipollone, upon that — those discussions with Mr. Philbin, with Greg Jacobs, what was your assessment as to what the vice president could or could not do in the general session?"

Pat Cipollone: "What was my assessment about what he could or couldn't do?"

Unknown: "Yes, your view of the issues?"

Pat Cipollone: "My view was that a vice president had — didn't have the legal authority to do anything except what he did."

Unknown: "They've both told us, Mr. Philbin and Mr. Jacob, that they looked very closely at the Eastman memos, the Eastman theory, and thought that it had no basis, that it was not a strategy that the president should pursue. It sounds like that's consistent with your impression as well."

Pat Cipollone: "My impression would have been informed, certainly, by them."

Stephanie Murphy: "Campaign senior adviser Jason Miller told us that Mr. Cipollone thought John Eastman's theories were nutty, something Mr. Cipollone wouldn't refute."

[multimedia]
Unknown: "We've received testimony from various people about this. One was Jason Miller, who was a campaign — said that the way it was communicated to me was that Pat Cipollone thought the idea was nutty, and at one point confronted Eastman, basically with the same sentiment, that –"

Pat Cipollone: "I don't have a reason to contradict what he said."

Stephanie Murphy: "On January 4th, John Eastman went to the White House to meet with the president and vice president. Mr. Cipollone tried to participate in this meeting, but he was apparently turned away."

[multimedia]
Unknown: "You didn't go to the meeting in the Oval Office where Eastman met with the president and the vice president. Do you know — do you remember why you didn't personally attend?"

Pat Cipollone: "I did walk to that meeting and I did go into the Oval Office with the idea of attending that meeting. And then I ultimately did not attend that meeting."

Unknown: "Why not?"

Pat Cipollone: "The reasons for that are privileged."

Unknown: "Ok. Were you asked to not attend the meeting, or did you make a personal decision not to attend the meeting?"

Pat Cipollone: "Again, without getting into –"

Unknown: "Privilege."

Stephanie Murphy: "Recall that Greg Jacob, the vice president's counsel, stated that Mr. Eastman acknowledged he would lose 9 to 0 if his legal theory were challenged in the Supreme Court. Mr. Cipollone had reviewed Mr. Eastman's legal theory and expressed his view repeatedly that the vice president was right. He even offered to take the blame for the vice president's position."

[multimedia]
Pat Cipollone: "I thought that the vice president did not have the authority to do what

was being suggested under a proper reading of the law. I conveyed that."

Unknown: "Ok."

Pat Cipollone: "I think I actually — somebody, you know, in the vice president's — just blame me. This — you know, this is — I'm not a politician. You know, I don't — but, you know, I just said I'm a lawyer. This is my legal opinion. I — but let me tell you this. Can I say a word about the vice president, please? I think the vice president did the right thing.

"I think he did the courageous thing. I have a great deal of respect for Vice President Pence. I've worked with him very closely. I think he understood my opinion. I think he understood my opinion afterwards as well. I think he did a great service to this country. And I think I suggested to somebody that he should be get — given the Presidential Medal of Freedom for — for his actions."

Stephanie Murphy: "Earlier this year, a federal district — district court judge concluded that President Trump and Mr. Eastman, relying on Mr. Eastman's theory, more likely than not violated multiple federal criminal laws in their pressure campaign against the vice president. Also, recall earlier in this hearing we saw that Rudy Giuliani's team did not have actual evidence of fraud sufficient to change the result of the election.

"That's important because, as January 6th approached, the Republican members of the House and Senate were looking for reason to object to the electors, and no real evidence was ever given to them. And we know that Republican members of the House received a memorandum from the chairwoman of the House

Republican Caucus in the days before January 6th explaining in detail the many constitutional and legal problems with objections and describing the principal judicial rulings dismissing the claims of widespread fraud.

"But their plan to object to the certification of the election on January 6th went forward anyway. The next day, on January 5th, the day before the attack on the Capitol, tens of thousands of people converged on Washington. While certain close associates of President Trump privately expressed concerns about what would occur on January 6th, other members of the president's inner circle spoke with great anticipation about the events to come.

"The committee has learned from the White House phone logs that the president spoke to Steve Bannon, his close adviser, at least twice on January 5th. The first conversation they had lasted for 11 minutes. Listen to what Mr. Bannon said that day after the first call he had with the President."

[multimedia]

Steve Bannon: "All hell is going to break loose tomorrow. It's all converging and now we're on, as they say, the point of attack, right, the point of attack tomorrow. I'll tell you this, it's not going to happen like you think it's going to happen, Ok? It's going to be quite extraordinarily different. And all I can say is strap in."

Stephanie Murphy: "From those same phone logs, we know that the president and Mr. Bannon spoke again on the phone that evening, this time for six minutes. That same day, on the eve of January 6th, supporters of President Trump gathered in Washington, DC at another rally. This rally was held at Freedom Plaza, which is located near the White House and featured some of the speakers who Katrina Pierson and others deemed too extreme to share the stage with the president the next morning.

"And as this rally was underway, the president asked members of his staff to come to the Oval Office. Let's hear from the White House aides who were in the Oval Office that night."

[multimedia]

<u>Nicholas Luna</u>: "I was in the office — in the Oval Office, and he had asked me to open the door so that he could hear. I guess there was a concert or a — or something going on."

<u>Unknown</u>: "Did he say anything other than just open the door?"

<u>Nicholas Luna</u>: "He — he made a comment. I don't remember specifically what he said, but there is a lot of energy."

<u>Sarah Matthews</u>: "We walked in, the staff was kind of standing up and assembled along the wall, and the president was at the desk and Dan Scavino was on the couch. And the president was dictating a tweet that he wanted Scavino to send out. Then the president started talking about the rally the next day. He had the door of the Oval open to the Rose Garden because you could hear the crowd already assembled outside on the Ellipse.

"And they were playing music, and it was so loud that you could feel it shaking in the Oval. He was in a very good mood. And I say that because he had not been in a good mood for weeks leading up to that, and then it seemed like he was in a fantastic mood that evening."

<u>Judd Deere</u>: "He asked if — if members of Congress would be with him tomorrow."

<u>Unknown</u>: "And what did you understand by — meaning voting in his favor as opposed to physically with him or anything like that?"

<u>Judd Deere</u>: "Yeah, I took that to mean not voting to certify the election."

<u>Sarah Matthews</u>: "Then he did look to the staff and ask for ideas of how — if I recall, he said that we could make the RINOs do the right thing is the way he phrased it. And no one spoke up initially, because I think everyone was trying to process what that — he meant by that."

<u>Shealah Craighead</u>: "The president was making notes that — talking then about we should go up to the Capitol, what's the best route to go to the Capitol."

<u>Judd Deere</u>: "I said he should focus on policy accomplishments. I didn't mention 2020."

<u>Unknown</u>: "What was his response?"

<u>Judd Deere</u>: "He acknowledged that and said we've had a lot, something along those lines. And — but then he fairly quickly move to how fired up the crowd is, was going to be."

<u>Unknown</u>: "And what did he say about it?"

<u>Judd Deere</u>: "Just that they were — they were fired up. They were angry. They feel like the election's been stolen, the election was rigged."

Unknown: "Did he give you any indication of how he knew that the crowd was fired up or angry?"

Judd Deere: "He continued to reference being able to hear them outside."

Stephanie Murphy: "Through the open door of the Oval Office, the president could hear the sound of the crowd and the music at the rally at the Freedom Plaza. And these are some of the things that they were saying there at the plaza, just blocks from where the president sat that evening excited for the next day."

[multimedia]

Roger Stone: "This is nothing less than an epic struggle for the future of this country, between dark and light, between the Godly and the godless, between good and evil. And we will win this fight or America would step off into a thousand years of darkness."

Michael Flynn: "Tomorrow, tomorrow, trust me, the American people that are standing on the soil that we are standing on tonight, and they're going to be standing on this soil tomorrow, this is soil that we have fought over, fought for, and we will fight for in the future. The members — the members of Congress, the members of the House of Representatives, the members of the — of the United States Senate, those of — those of you who are feeling weak tonight, those of you that don't have the moral fiber in your body, get some tonight because tomorrow we the people are going to be here.

"And we want you to know that we will not stand for a lie. We will not stand for a lie."

Ali Alexander: "I want them to know that 1776 is always an option. [Cheering] These degenerates in the deep state are going to give us what we want or we are going to shut this country down. [Cheering]"

Alex Jones: "It's 1776, 1776, 1776, 1776."

Stephanie Murphy: "At 5:05 PM, as the Freedom Plaza rally was underway just blocks away, President Trump tweeted, Washington is being inundated with people who don't want to see an election victory stolen by emboldened radical left Democrats. Our country has had enough. They won't take it anymore. To the crowds gathering in DC he added, we hear you and love you from the Oval Office.

"The committee has learned that on January 5th, there were serious concerns at Twitter about the anticipated violence the next day. Listen to what the Twitter witness told us about their desperate efforts to get Twitter to do something."

[multimedia]
Unknown: "What was your — your gut feeling on the night of January 5th? I believe I sent a Slack message to someone that said something along the lines of when people are shooting each other tomorrow, I will try and rest in the knowledge that we tried. And so, I went to — I don't know that I slept that night, to be honest with you. I — I was on pins and needles because, again, for — for months I had been begging and anticipating and attempting to raise the reality that if nothing — if we made no intervention into what I saw occurring, people were going to die. And on January 5th, I realized no intervention was coming. No — there — and even as — as hard as I had tried to create one or implement one, there was

**nothing and we were — we were at the whims
and the mercy of a violent crowd that was
locked and loaded.**

**"And just for the record, this was content that
was echoing statements by the former
president, but also Proud Boys and other
known violent extremist groups? Yeah."**

<u>Stephanie Murphy</u>: "There were also concerns among
members of Congress. We have a recently released
recording of a conversation that took place among
Republican members in the US Capitol on the eve of
January 6th. This is Republican Congresswoman Debbie
Lesko from Arizona, who led some of the unfounded
objections to the election results."

[multimedia]
<u>Debbie Lesko</u>: **"I also asked leadership to come
up with a safety plan for members. I'm
actually very concerned about this, because we
have who knows how many hundreds of
thousands of people coming here. We have
Antifa. We also have, quite honestly, Trump
supporters who actually believe that we are
going to overturn the election.**

**"And when that doesn't happen, most likely
will not happen, they are going to go nuts."**

<u>Stephanie Murphy</u>: "That same evening, as President
Trump listened to the rally from the Oval Office, he was
also working on his speech to be delivered the next day.
And based on documents we've received from the
National Archives, including multiple drafts of the
President's speech as well as from witness testimony, we
understand how that speech devolved into a call to action
and a call to fight.

"One of the first edits President Trump made to his speech was to incorporate his 5:05 pm tweet, revising his speech to say, 'all of us are here today, do not want to see our election victory stolen by emboldened radical left Democrats. Our country has had enough. We will not take it anymore.' He also added, 'together we will stop the steal'. President Trump's edits continued into the morning of January 6th. And as you can see from the President's daily diary here, the President spoke to his chief speechwriter, Stephen Miller, for over 25 minutes that morning.

"Following his call with Mr. Miller, President Trump inserted for the first time a line in his speech that said, quote, 'and we will see whether Mike Pence enters history as a truly great and courageous leader. All he has to do is refer the illegally submitted electoral votes back to the states that were given false and fraudulent information where they want to recertify'. No prior version of this speech had referenced Vice President Pence or his role during the joint session on January 6th. These last minute edits by President Trump to his speech were part of the President's pressure campaign against his own Vice President.

"But not everyone wanted these lines regarding the Vice President included in the President's speech, including White House lawyer, Eric Hirschmann."

[multimedia]
<u>Unknown</u>: "Did you ever speak to anybody in the White House at the time about this disagreement between the President and the Vice President other than the President based on the objection from your counsel?"

<u>Stephen Miller</u>: "Maybe had a brief conversation about it with Eric Hirschmann."

Unknown: "Tell me about that. What do you remember him saying to you about this disagreement?"

Stephen Miller: "I just remember him saying that — that he had a — don't — get this wrong — sort of something to the effect of thinking that it would be counterproductive I think he thought to — to discuss the matter publicly."

Unknown: "So it came up in the context of editing the President's speech on January the sixth."

Stephen Miller: "I just came up in the conversation where Eric knew what was in the speech and so he had a sidebar with me about it."

Stephanie Murphy: "And so the speechwriters took that advice and removed the lines about Vice President Pence. And later that morning at 11:20 am President Trump had a phone call with the Vice President. And as the committee detailed in an earlier hearing, that phone call was by all accounts tense and heated. During this call, the Vice President told the President that he would not attempt to change the outcome of the election.

"In response, the President called the Vice President of the United States a wimp and other derogatory words. As you can see in this email, after Vice President Pence told President Trump that he would not unilaterally deliver him a second term in office, the speechwriters were directed to re-insert the Mike Pence lines.

"Here is how one of the speechwriters described President Trump's last minute change to the speech."

[multimedia]

Vincent Haley: "And as I recall, there was a very tough — a tough sentence about the Vice President that was — that was — was added."

Stephanie Murphy: "President Trump wanted to use his speech to attack Vice President Pence in front of a crowd of thousands of angry supporters who had been led to believe the election was stolen. When President Trump arrived at the Ellipse to deliver his speech, he was still worked up from his call with Vice President Pence.

"And although Ivanka Trump would not say so, her chief of staff gave the committee some insight into the President's frustration."

[multimedia]
Unknown: "It's been reported that you ultimately decided to attend the rally because you hoped that you would calm the President and keep the event on an even keel. Is that accurate?"

Ivanka Trump: "No, I don't know who said that or where that came from."

Unknown: "What did she share with you about why it was concerning that her father was upset or agitated after that call with Vice President Pence in relation to the Ellipse rally? Why did that matter? Why did he have to be calmed down, I should say."

Julie Radford: "Well, she shared that he had called the Vice President a not — an [expletive] word, I think that bothered her. And I think she could tell based on the conversations and what was going on in the office that he was angry and upset and people were providing this information. And she felt

**like she might be able to help calm the
situation down at least before he went on to
stage."**

Stephanie Murphy: "The President did go on stage and
then he gave the speech that he wanted to give. It included
the formal changes he had requested the night before and
in that morning. But also many important last minute adlib
changes. A single scripted reference in the speech to Mike
Pence became eight. A single scripted reference to rally
goers marching to the Capitol became four.

"With President Trump adlibbing that he would be joining
the protesters at the Capitol. Added throughout his speech
were references to fighting and the need for people to have
courage and to be strong. The word peacefully was in the
staff written script and used only once. Here are some of
these adlib changes that the President made to his speech."

[multimedia]

**Donald Trump: "Because you'll never take
back our country with weakness. You have to
show strength and you have to be strong. So I
hope Mike has the courage to do what he has
to do. And I hope he doesn't listen to the
rhinos and the stupid people that he's listening
to. We fight like hell. And if you don't fight
like hell, you're not going to have a country
anymore.**

**"But we're going to try and give our
Republicans, the weak ones, because the strong
ones don't need any of our help, we're going to
try and give them the kind of pride and
boldness that they need to take back our
country. So let's walk down Pennsylvania
Avenue —"**

Stephanie Murphy: "White House counsel, Pat Cipollone, and his deputy did not attend the speech and they were concerned that the statements in the speech about the election were false. In fact, the message that President Trump delivered that day was built on a foundation of lies. He lied to his supporters that the election was stolen.

"He stoked their anger. He called for them to fight for him. He directed them to the US Capitol. He told them he would join them, and his supporters believed him and many headed towards the Capitol. As a result, people died. People were injured. Many of his supporters' lives will never be the same. President Trump's former campaign manager, Brad Parscale, recognized the impact of the speech immediately and this is what he said on January 6th in excerpts from text messages to Katrina Pierson.

"Mr. Parscale said, quote, 'this is about Trump pushing for uncertainty in our country'. 'A sitting President asking for civil war.' And then when he said, 'this week I feel guilty for helping him win'. Katrina Pierson responded, 'you did what you felt right at the time and therefore it was right'. Mr. Parscale added, 'yeah, but a woman is dead'. And, 'yeah, if I was Trump and I knew my rhetoric killed someone'. When Ms. Pierson replied, 'it wasn't the rhetoric'. Mr. Pascal said, 'Katrina, yes, it was'. Thank you Mr. Chairman, I yield back."

Bennie Thompson: "Gentlelady yields back. We're joined today by Mr. Jason Van Tatenhove and Mr. Stephen Ayres. Mr. Tatenhove is an artist and journal — journalist. He's a former spokesman of the Oath Keepers and a former close associate of Elmer Stewart Rhodes, the founder and President of the Oath Keepers, who has been charged with seditious conspiracy in relation to the Capitol attack.

"Mr. Van Tatenhove broke with the Oath Keepers and has since spoken out forcefully against a violent group. Mr. Ayres is a former supporter of President Trump. He answered the President's call to come to Washington DC on January 6th. He marched to the Capitol on the President's orders. He pleaded guilty last month to disorderly and disruptive conduct at the Capitol.

"Mr. Ayres, who no longer supports President Trump, came forward voluntarily to share his story as a warning. I will now swear in our witnesses. The witnesses will please stand and raise their right hand. Do you swear or affirm on the penalty of perjury that the testimony you're about to give is the truth, the whole truth, and nothing but the truth.

"So help you God."

Unknown: [off-mic]

Bennie Thompson: "Thank you. You may be seated. Let the record reflect that the witnesses answered in the affirmative. I recognize myself for questions. Today we've discussed how President Trump summoned an angry mob of supporters to Washington, DC, many of whom came prepared to do battle against police and politicians alike.

"We're fortunate enough to be joined by two witnesses who can help us understand who was in the mob that day. Both hard core violent extremists like the Oath Keepers and Proud Boys and average Trump supporters swept up in the fervor of the day. Mr. Van Tatenhove, can you help us understand who the Oath Keepers are?"

Jason Van Tatenhove: "I can. Thank you. My time with the Oath Keepers began back at Bondy Ranch with that first standoff when I went to cover them as an independent journalist. I then subsequently covered two more standoffs, the Sugar Pine Mine standoff and the White Hope Mine standoff. It was at that time that I was offered a job as national media director and an associate editor for the Web page.

"So I spent a few years with the Oath Keepers and I can tell you that they may not like to call themselves a militia, but they are. They're a violent militia. And they are largely Stewart Rhodes. They — and I think rather than try to use words, I think the — the best illustration for what the Oath Keepers are happened January 6th when we saw that stacked military formation going up the stairs of our Capitol. I saw radicalization that started with my beginning of my time with them and continued over a period of time as the member base and who it was that Stewart Rhodes was courting drifted further and further right into the alt right world into white nationalists and even straight up racists. And it came to a point where I could no longer continue to — to work for them, but the Oath Keepers are — are a dangerous militia that that is in large part fed by the ego and drive of Stewart Rhodes to at times seemed to see himself as this paramilitary leader.

"I think that drove a lot of it. So in my opinion, the Oath Keepers are a very dangerous organization."

Bennie Thompson: "Well, thank you very much. You've talked a little bit about that danger. So what is the Oath Keepers' vision for America and why should Americans be concerned about it?"

Jason Van Tatenhove: "I think we saw a glimpse of what the vision of the Oath Keepers is on January 6th. It doesn't necessarily include the rule of law. It doesn't necessarily include — it includes violence. It includes trying to — to get their way through lies, through deceit, through intimidation, and through the perpetration of violence, the swaying of — of people who may not know better through lies and rhetoric and propaganda that can get swept up in these moments.

"And I will admit I was swept up at one point as well too. But — and I don't know if that answers the question."

Bennie Thompson: "Well, it does. And you talk about being swept up. So at what point did you break with the Oath Keepers?"

Jason Van Tatenhove: "There came a point — there were many red flags and I probably should have broke with them much earlier than I did. But the straw that broke the camel's back really came when I walked into a grocery store. We were living up in the very remote town of Eureka, Montana and there was a group of core members of the group of the Oath Keepers and some associates, and they were having a conversation at that public area where they were talking about how the Holocaust was not real.

"And that was for me something I just could not abide. And you know, we were not — we were not wealthy people at all. We were barely surviving. And it didn't matter — I went home to my wife and my kids, and I told them that I've got to walk away at this point. I don't know how we're going to survive or where we're going to go or what we're going to do, but I just can no longer continue, and put in my resignation."

Bennie Thompson: "Thank you very much. Mr. Ayres, there were many people in the crowd that day on January 6, including you, who were not part of an extremist group. I'd like to start by having you tell the American people a little bit about yourself. Can you tell us about your life before January 6th?"

Stephen Ayres: "Yeah. Basically, nothing but a family man and a working man. Worked at the company, a cabinet company up in Northeast Ohio for going on 20 years. You know, family is my life. You know, I was a supervisor there, so that that took up a lot of my other — you know, a lot of my free time. Other than that, with my family camping, playing basketball, playing games with my son."

Bennie Thompson: "Just what any ordinary American citizen, family man, would do."

Stephen Ayres: "Yeah, exactly."

Bennie Thompson: "So this committee has reviewed thousands of hours of surveillance footage from January 6. During this review, we identified you entering the Capitol as we see in this video. Mr. Ayres, why did you decide to come to Washington on January 6th?"

Stephen Ayres: "For me, for me personally, you know — I was, you know, pretty hardcore into the social media, Facebook, Twitter, Instagram. I followed, you know, President Trump, you know, on all the websites, you know. He basically put out, you know, come to the Stop the Steal rally, you know, and I felt like I needed to be down here."

Bennie Thompson: "So — so you basically learned about the rally on social media, and at some point made a decision to come to Washington."

Stephen Ayres: "Yeah, yeah. I had some friends I found out were coming down. I just hopped — you know, hopped on with them right at the tail end when I found out, and Came down here with them."

Bennie Thompson: "Thank you very much. The Chair recognizes the Vice Chair Ms. Cheney of Wyoming with any questions that she may have."

Liz Cheney: "Thank you very much, Mr. Chairman. Mr. Ayers, when you entered the Capitol last year, did you believe that the election had been stolen? At that time, yeah. You know, everything that I was — I was seeing online, I definitely believed that that's exactly what — that was the case. And when you heard from President Trump that the election was stolen, how did that make you feel?"

Stephen Ayres: "Oh, I was, you know, I was very upset, as were most of his supporters. You know, that's basically what got me to come down here."

Liz Cheney: "And do you still believe the election was stolen?"

Stephen Ayres: "Not so much now. I got away from all the social media when January 6 happened, basically deleted it all. You know, I started doing my own research and everything. And for me — for me for something like that to be that — to actually for that to actually take place, it's too big, you know. There'd be — there's no way you can keep something like that quiet, as big as something like that.

"You know, with all the, you know, all the lawsuits being shot down one after another, that — that was mainly what convinced me."

Liz Cheney: "Well, and I think that's very important. And we've also talked about today and in previous hearings the extent to which the President himself was told that the election hadn't been stolen, by his Justice Department, by his White House counsel, by his campaign. Would it have made a difference to you to know that President Trump himself had no evidence of widespread fraud?"

Stephen Ayres: "Oh, definitely, you know. Who knows, I may not have come down here then, you know."

Liz Cheney: "Thank you very much. Mr. Chairman, I yield back."

Bennie Thompson: "The gentlelady yields back. The chair recognizes the gentlewoman from Florida, Ms. Murphy."

Stephanie Murphy: "Thank you. Mr. Chairman. You know, earlier today we showed how Donald Trump's December 19th tweet summoned both extremist groups as well as rank and file supporters of President Trump to come to Washington, DC, average Americans. He — he told them to, quote, be there, will be wild; and they came. We showed how Mr. President — how President Trump repeatedly told them fight, fight, fight, and they marched to the Capitol.

"Mr. Ayres, you were in that crowd at the rally, and then the crowd that marched to the Capitol. When you arrived on the Ellipse that morning, were you planning on going to the Capitol?"

Stephen Ayres: "No, we didn't actually plan to go down there. You know, we went basically to see the Stop the Steal rally and that was it."

Stephanie Murphy: "So why did you decide to march to the Capitol?"

Stephen Ayres: "Well, basically, you know, the President got everybody riled up and told everybody to head on down. So we basically was just following what he said."

Stephanie Murphy: "After the President's speech as you're marching down to the Capitol, how did you feel?"

Stephen Ayres: "I was, you know, I'm angry. You know, after everything that was basically said in the speech. You know, a lot of the stuff he said he already put out in tweets. I've already seen it and heard it before. So, I mean, I was already worked up and so were most of the people there."

Stephanie Murphy: "So as you started marching, did you think there was still a chance the election would be overturned?"

Stephen Ayres: "Yeah, at that time I did, you know, because everybody was kind of like in the hope that, you know, Vice President Pence was not going to certify the election. You know, also the whole time on our way down there, we kept hearing about this big reveal I remember us talking about, and we kind of thought maybe that was it. So that hope was there."

Stephanie Murphy: "Did you think that the President would be marching with you?"

Stephen Ayres: "Yeah, I think everybody thought he was going to be coming down. You know, he said it in his speech, you know, kind of like he's going to be there with us. So, I mean, I think — I believed it."

Stephanie Murphy: "I understand. We know that you illegally entered the Capitol that afternoon and then left the Capitol area later on. What made you decide to leave?"

Stephen Ayres: "Basically, when President Trump put his tweet out. We literally left right after that come out. You know, to me if he would have done that earlier in the day, 1:30, I — you know, we wouldn't be in this — maybe we wouldn't be in this bad of a situation or something."

Stephanie Murphy: "Thank you. Mr. Chairman, I yield back."

Bennie Thompson: "The Chair recognizes the gentleman from Maryland, Mr. Raskin."

Jamie Raskin: "Thank you, Mr. Chairman. Mr. Van Tatenhove, in the run-up to January 6, Stewart Rhodes publicly implored President Trump to invoke the

Insurrection Act, the 1807 law that allows the President to call up militias to put down a rebellion against the United States. And I want to get your thoughts about this in the context of your prior relationship with Stewart Rhodes.

"I understand that you had conversations with Rhodes about the Insurrection Act. Why was he so fixated on that, and what did he think it would enable the Oath Keepers to do?"

Jason Van Tatenhove: "Well, I think it gave him a sense of legitimacy, that it was a path forward to move forward with his goals and agendas. I think we need to quit mincing words and just talk about truths, and what it was going to be was an armed revolution. I mean, people died that day. Law enforcement officers died this day. There was a gallows set up in front of the Capitol. This could have been the spark that started a new civil war, and no one would have won there. That would have been good for no one. He was always looking for ways to legitimize what he was doing, whether by wrapping it in the trappings of, it's not a militia, it's a community preparedness team.

"We're not a militia, we're an educational outreach group. It's a veterans support group. But again, we've got to stop with this — this dishonesty and the mincing of words and just call things for what they are. You know, he's a militia leader. He had these grand visions of being a paramilitary leader, and the Insurrection Act would have given him a path forward with that.

"You know, the fact that the President was communicating, whether directly or indirectly messaging, you know, kind of that gave him the nod. And all I can do is thank the gods that things did not go any worse that day."

Jamie Raskin: "What did the Oath Keepers see in President Trump?"

Jason Van Tatenhove: "They saw a path forward that would have legitimacy. They saw opportunity, I think, in my opinion, to become a paramilitary force, you know."

Jamie Raskin: "Last week, the Department of Justice indicated that it has evidence of the Oath Keepers bringing not just firearms but explosives to Washington ahead of January 6th. And the committee has also learned that Stewart Rhodes stopped to buy weapons on his way to Washington, and shipped roughly $7,000 worth of tactical gear to a January 6th rally planner in Virginia before the attack.

"Did you ever hear Rhodes discuss committing violence against elected political leaders?"

Jason Van Tatenhove: "Yeah, I mean, that went back from the very beginning of my tenure. One of the first assignments that he brought to me, wanting me to do as more of a graphic artist function was to create a deck of cards. You may remember back to the conflict in the Middle East where our own military created a deck of cards, which was a who's who of kind of the — the key players on the other side that they wanted to take out.

"And Stewart was very intrigued by that notion and influenced by it, I think. And he wanted me to create a deck of cards that would include different politicians, judges, including up to Hillary Clinton as the queen of hearts. This was a project that I refused to do. But from the very start, we saw that. There was always the — the push for military training, including there were — there were — there were courses in that community that went over explosives training.

"So, yeah, this all falls in line."

Jamie Raskin: "Mr. Van Tatenhove, you say in your very thoughtful written testimony that we received today that you fear what the next election cycle will bring. And you also say that we have been exceedingly lucky, in that we have not seen more bloodshed so far. I wonder if you would elaborate on those two statements."

Jason Van Tatenhove: "I think, as far as the luck goes, we've had the potential from Bundy Ranch on. I mean, being boots on the ground at these — these standoffs, and they were standoffs, where there were firearms pointed across lines at federal law enforcement agencies. You know, whatever it may be with that particular standoff.

"But I do — I think we've gotten exceedingly lucky that more bloodshed did not happen, because the potential has been there from the start. And we got very lucky that the loss of life was — and as tragic as it is that we saw on January 6th, the potential was so much more.

"Again, all we have to look at is the iconic images of that day with the gallows set up for Mike Pence, for the Vice President of the United States, you know.

"And I do fear for this next election cycle, because who knows what that might bring? If — if a president that's willing to try to instill and encourage to whip up a civil war amongst his followers using lies and deceit and snake oil, and regardless of the human impact, what else is he going to do if he gets elected again?

"All bets are off at that point, and that's a scary notion. I have three daughters; I have a granddaughter. And I fear for the world that they will inherit if we do not start holding these — these people to account."

Jamie Raskin: "Thank you for your testimony, Mr. Van Tatenhove. Mr. Ayres, I first want to ask you about what finally caused you to leave on January the 6th. We know that the medieval style combat with our police, the occupation of the building, this was going on for several hours until the President issued at 4:17 a tweet, I believe that included a video, telling people to go home.

"Did you see that, and did that have any effect on what you were doing?"

Stephen Ayres: "Well, when we were there, as soon as that come out, everybody started talking about it and that's — it seemed like it started to disperse. You know, some of the crowd, obviously, you know, once we got back to the hotel room, we seen that it was still going on. But it definitely dispersed a lot of the crowd."

Jamie Raskin: "And did you leave at that point?"

Stephen Ayres: "Yeah, we did. Yeah, we left."

Jamie Raskin: "So, in other words, that was the key moment when you decided to leave when President Trump told people to go home."

Stephen Ayres: "Yeah, yeah, we left right when that come out."

Jamie Raskin: "You were not a member of an organized group like the Oath Keepers or the Proud Boys, as most of the crowd wasn't. I wonder on January 6th, was it your view that these far-right groups like the Oath Keepers and Proud Boys and Three Percenters and others were on your side? Did you have any reservations about marching with them and rallying with them?"

Stephen Ayres: "Well, I definitely didn't have a problem, you know. I was probably following them online myself. You know, I liked — I thought, you know, hey, they're on our team; good. That's how I kind of looked at it at the time, you know, like I didn't have a problem with it. I thought it was a good thing."

Jamie Raskin: "I'm interested in hearing about what's happened to you since the events of January 6th. You told the vice chair that you no longer believe Trump's big lie about the election, but that's what brought you originally to Washington. Looking back on it now, how do you reflect on the role that you played in the crowd that day, and what is going on in your life?"

Stephen Ayres: "Basically, you know, I lost my job. Since this all happened, you know, pretty much sold my house. So everything that happened with the charges, you know, thank God, a lot of them did get dismissed because I was just holding my phone. But at the same time, I was there. So, I mean, it definitely — it changed my life, you know, and not for the good.

"Definitely not for the, you know, for the better. Yeah, I mean, really all I can say."

Jamie Raskin: "Well, President Trump is still promoting the big lie about the election. How does that make you feel?"

Stephen Ayres: "It makes me mad because I — I was hanging on every word he was saying. Everything he was putting out, I was following it. I mean, if I was doing it, hundreds of thousands or millions of other people are doing it, or maybe even still doing it. It's like he just said about that, you know, you got people still following and doing that.

"Who knows what the next election could come out, you know. It could end up being down the same path we are right now. I mean, just don't know."

Jamie Raskin: "Mr. Ayres, I see that your wife has joined you today, and welcome to Washington. We know this has been very difficult on you both and your family. What lessons finally do you want the American people to learn from the way you and your family have suffered as a result of these events?"

Stephen Ayres: "The biggest thing is I consider myself a family man, and I love my country. I don't think any one man is bigger than either one of those. I think that's what needed to be taken, you know. People dive into the politics, and for me I felt like I had, you know, like horse blinders on. I was — I was locked in the whole time. Biggest thing for me is take the blinders off, make sure you step back and see what's going on before it's too late."

Jamie Raskin: "Well, I want to thank you for your testimony and for appearing, both of you, today. And Mr. Chairman, I yield back to you."

Bennie Thompson: "The gentleman yields back. I want to thank our witnesses for joining us today. The members of the select committee may have additional questions for today's witnesses, and we ask that you respond expeditiously in writing to those questions. Without objections, members will be permitted ten business days to submit statements for the record, including opening remarks and additional questions for the witnesses.

"Without objection, the Chair recognizes the gentleman from Maryland, Mr. Raskin, for a closing statement."

Jamie Raskin: "Thank you, Mr. Chairman. When Donald Trump sent out his tweet, he became the first President ever to call for a crowd to descend on the capital city to block the constitutional transfer of power. He set off an explosive chain reaction among his followers, but no one mobilized more quickly than the dangerous extremists that we've looked at today.

"Seizing upon his invitation to fight, they assembled their followers for an insurrectionary showdown against Congress and the Vice President. On January 6, Trump knew the crowd was angry. He knew the crowd was armed. He sent them to the Capitol anyway. You might imagine that our founders would have been shocked to learn that an American President would one day come to embrace and excuse political violence against our own institutions, or knowingly send an armed mob to attack the Capitol to usurp the will of the people. But, you know, Mr. Chairman, the founders were pretty wise about certain things. And at the start of the republic, they actually warned everyone about Donald Trump. Not by name, of course, but in the course of advising about the certain prospect that ambitious politicians would try to mobilize violent mobs to tear down our own institutions in service of their insatiable ambitions.

"In the very first Federalist Paper, Alexander Hamilton observed that history teaches that opportunistic politicians who desire to rule at all costs will begin first as demagogues, pandering to the angry and malignant passions of the crowd, but then end up as tyrants, trampling the freedoms and the rights of the people.

"A violent insurrection to overturn an election is not an abstract thing, as we've heard. Hundreds of people were bloodied, injured, and wounded in the process, including more than 150 police officers, some of them sitting in this room today. I want to give you an update on one officer who was badly wounded in the attack and is well known to the members of this committee, because he testified before us last year.

"Sergeant Aquilino Gonell is an Army veteran who spent a year on active combat duty in the Iraq war and then 16 years on the Capitol force. Nothing he ever saw in combat in Iraq, he has said, prepared him for the insurrection where he was savagely beaten, punched, pushed, kicked, shoved, stomped, and sprayed with chemical irritants, along with other officers, by members of a mob carrying hammers, knives, batons, and police shields, taken by force and wielding the American flag against police officers as a dangerous weapon.

"Last month on June 28th, Sergeant Gonell's team of doctors told him that permanent injuries he has suffered to his left shoulder and right foot now make it impossible for him to continue as a police officer. He must leave policing for good and figure out the rest of his life. Sergeant Gonell, we wish you and your family all the best.

"We are here for you. We salute you for your valor, your eloquence, and your beautiful commitment to America. I wonder what former President Trump would say to someone like Sergeant Gonell who must now go about remaking his life. I wonder if he could even understand what motivates a patriot like Sergeant Gonell. In his inaugural address, Trump introduced one commanding image, American carnage. Although that turn of phrase explained little about our country before he took office, it turned out to be an excellent prophecy of what his rage would come to visit on our people. Mr. Ayres just described how the trust he placed in President Trump as a camp follower derailed his life and nearly wrecked his reputation and his family.

"A few weeks ago, we heard Shaye Moss and her mother Ruby Freeman, Speaker Rusty Bowers from Arizona, and Georgia Secretary of State Brad Raffensperger describe how hate-filled intimidation campaigns by Trump and his followers made them prisoners in their homes, and drove their stress and anxiety to soaring new heights when they refused to do Trump's bidding.

"American carnage, that's Donald Trump's true legacy. His desire to overthrow the people's election and seize the presidency interrupted the counting of Electoral College votes for the first time in American history, nearly toppled the constitutional order, and brutalized hundreds and hundreds of people. The Watergate break-in was like a Cub Scout meeting compared to this assault on our people and our institutions.

"Mr. Chairman, these hearings have been significant for us and for millions of Americans. And our hearing next week will be a profound moment of reckoning for America. But the crucial thing is the next step, what this committee — what all of us will do to fortify our democracy against coups, political violence, and campaigns to steal elections away from the people.

"Unlike Mr. Ayres and Mr. Van Tatenhove, people who have recovered and evolved from their descent into the hell of fanaticism, Donald Trump has only expanded his big lie. To cover January 6th itself, he asserts the insurrection was the real election, and the election was the real insurrection. He says his mob greeted our police officers on January 6th with hugs and kisses.

"He threatens to take one of America's two major political parties with him down the road to authoritarianism. And it is Abraham Lincoln's party, no less. The political scientists tell us that authoritarian parties have two essential features in common, in history and around the world. They do not accept the results of democratic elections when they lose, and they embrace political violence as legitimate.

"And the problem — and the problem of incitement to political violence has only grown more serious in the Internet age, as we have just heard. But this is not the problem of one party; it is the problem of the whole country now. American democracy, Mr. Chairman, is a precious inheritance, something rare in the history of the world and even on earth today.

"Constitutional democracy is the silver frame, as Lincoln put it, upon which the golden apple of freedom rests. We need to defend both our democracy and our freedom with everything we have, and declare that this American carnage ends here and now. In a world of resurgent authoritarianism and racism and anti-Semitism, let's all hang tough for American democracy.

"Thank you, Mr. Chairman. I yield back."

Bennie Thompson: "The gentleman yields back. Without objection, the Chair recognizes the gentlewoman from Florida, Ms. Murphy, for a closing statement."

Stephanie Murphy: "Thank you, Mr. Chairman. At one of our first hearings, Chairman Thompson explained that the members of this committee would not spend much time talking about ourselves. Rather, we would let the evidence play the leading role. And the Chairman was right, because this isn't about promoting ourselves as Individuals.

"It's about protecting the country we love. And it's about preserving what actually makes America great: the rule of law, free and fair elections, and the peaceful transfer of power from one elected leader to the next. But if I may say a word about myself and why I'm proud to serve on this committee, I'm the only member of this committee who was not blessed to be born an American. I was born in Vietnam after the Vietnam War, and my family and I fled a communist government and were rescued by the US Navy, and were given sanctuary in America. My patriotism is rooted in my gratitude for America's grace and generosity. I love this country. On January 6th, four decades after my family fled a place where political power was seized through violence, I was in the United States Capitol fleeing my fellow Americans.

"Members of the angry mob had been lied to by a President and other powerful people who tried to convince them without evidence that the election had been stolen from them. Some of them then tried to use physical violence to overturn the outcome of a free and fair election. Our committee's overriding objective is to fight fiction with facts; to create a full account for the American people and for the historical record; to tell the truth of what happened and why it happened; to make recommendations so it never happens again; to defend our democracy.

"To me, there's nothing more patriotic than that. Thank you. Mr. Chairman, I yield back."

Bennie Thompson: "The gentlelady yields back. Without objection, the Chair recognizes the gentlewoman from Wyoming, Ms. Cheney, for a closing statement."

Liz Cheney: "Thank you very much, Mr. Chairman. Mr. Chairman, let me put what you have seen today in a broader context. At the very outset of our hearings, we described several elements of President Trump's multipart plan to overturn the 2020 election. Our hearings have now covered all but one of those elements, an organized campaign to persuade millions of Americans of a falsehood that the 2020 election was stolen by widespread fraud; a corrupt effort to pressure Vice President Pence to refuse to count electoral votes; an effort to corrupt the US Department of Justice; efforts to pressure state election officials and legislators to change state election results; a scheme to create and submit fake electoral slates from multiple states. And today, you saw how President Trump summoned a mob to Washington for January 6th, and then knowing that that mob was armed, directed that mob to the United States Capitol. Every one of these elements of the planning for January 6th is an independently serious matter. They were all ultimately focused on overturning the election, and they all have one other thing in common.

"Donald Trump participated in each, substantially and personally. He oversaw or directed the activity of those involved. Next week, we will return to January 6th itself. As we have shown in prior hearings, Donald Trump and his legal team led by Rudy Giuliani were working on January 6th — delay or halt Congress's counting of electoral votes.

"The mob attacking and invading the Capitol on that afternoon of January 6th was achieving that result. And for multiple hours, Donald Trump refused to intervene to stop it. He would not instruct the mob to leave or condemn the violence. He would not order them to evacuate the Capitol and disperse. The many pleas for help from Congress did no good.

"His staff insisted that President Trump call off the attack. He would not. Here are a few of the many things you will hear next week from Mr. Cipollone."

[multimedia]
Unknown: "[off-mic]— is that right?"

Pat Cipollone: "I was. And others were as well."

Unknown: "Ok. Was it necessary for you to continue to push for a statement directing people to leave all the way through that period of time until it was ultimately issued after –"

Pat Cipollone: "I felt it was my obligation to continue to push for that and others felt that it was their obligation as well."

Unknown: "Would it have been possible at any moment for the President to walk down to the podium in the briefing room and — and talk to the nation at any time between when you first

gave him that advice at 2:00 and 4:17 when the video statement went out? Would that have been possible?"

<u>Pat Cipollone</u>: "Would it have been possible?"

<u>Unknown</u>: "Yes."

<u>Pat Cipollone</u>: "Yes, it would have been possible."

<u>**Liz Cheney**</u>: "And you will hear that Donald Trump never picked up the phone that day to order his administration to help. This is not ambiguous. He did not call the military. His Secretary of Defense received no order. He did not call his attorney general. He did not talk to the Department of Homeland Security. Mike Pence did all of those things.

"Donald Trump did not. We will walk through the events of January 6th next week minute by minute. And one more item, after our last hearing, President Trump tried to call a witness in our investigation. A witness you have not yet seen in these hearings. That person declined to answer or respond to President Trump's call and instead alerted their lawyer to the call.

"Their lawyer alerted us and this committee has supplied that information to the Department of Justice. Let me say one more time, we will take any effort to influence witness testimony very seriously. Thank you, Mr. Chairman. I yield back."

<u>**Bennie Thompson**</u>: "Thank you. Gentlelady yields back. In my opening, I mentioned how we look to our leaders to serve as a failsafe if people in this country refuse to accept the results of an election. That's part of the way those in positions of public trust uphold their oath, how they show fidelity to the Constitution. In the run up to January 6th,

Donald Trump had an obligation to tell his supporters to accept the results of the election.

"Instead he urged them to further along the path toward mob violence. The idea of mob violence make me think of another sort of fail safe. All across this country, there are different ideas about what role the federal government should play in our lives. In fact, [untranslated] there are plenty of different ideas, but there are moments when the institutions of our federal government are the failsafe.

"I am from a part of the country where had it not been for the federal government and the Constitution my parents and many more Americans like them would have continued to be treated as second class citizens. The freedom to be able to vote without harassment, travel in relative safety, and dine and sleep where you choose is because we have a government that looks over the well-being of its citizens.

"This is especially important in moments of crisis. When we have a natural disaster that state governments can't handle on their own, when there's an emergency that's [requires] action by public health services or our military, we have a federal government. What happened on January 6, 2020 was another one of those moments in history that test the strength of our federal government.

"January 6th was an attack on our country. It was an attack on our democracy, on our Constitution. A sitting President with a violent mob trying to stop the peaceful transfer of power from one President to another. It still makes my blood boil to think of it. In a moment like that, what would you expect to see?

"You expect to see the President of the United States sitting behind the resolute desk in the Oval Office assuring the American people that the attack would be repelled and a threat would be dealt with. You would expect to be reassured that there was a failsafe. Instead the President of the United States sent the mob.

"He disregarded the advice of the people who had taken an oath to the Constitution. He oversaw a scheme aided by people whose loyalty was only to Donald Trump. There's nothing we can compare that to. There's nothing in our great nation's history that has ever come close to that sort of betrayal and dereliction.

"Thank goodness our system of government held in spite of a Commander in Chief who worked in opposition to what the Constitution desired. When this committee reconvenes, we'll tell the story of that supreme dereliction by the Commander in Chief, how close we came to a catastrophe for democracy, and how we remain in serious danger.

"The Chair requests those in the hearing room remain seated until the Capitol Police have escorted witnesses and members from the room. Without objection, the committee stands adjourned."

Made in the USA
Columbia, SC
16 March 2023

13899123R00048